KINGDOM GENEROSITY

DISCOVERING THE SECRET TO THE ABUNDANT LIFE

JACOB COKELY

BRANCH
&VINE
PUBLISHING

Hardcover: 978-1-969816-00-0
Paperback: 978-1-969816-01-7
Ebook: 978-1-969816-02-4

Printed in the United States of America.

SPECIAL THANKS

I'd like to thank my beautiful wife, Emma, and my son, Wess, for supporting me and giving me the space to write this book. I'd also like to thank my mom for always supporting and encouraging me.

CONTENTS

INTRODUCTION

When God nudged me to stop following the news, I obeyed without knowing why. I didn't have social media, so news became my outlet to unwind. I spent too much time keeping up with the news, but it was a habit and a passion. I said yes to God, and what followed was a vivid dream about kingdom generosity a week later. In my dream, people shared all the ways they showcased their skills, talents, and expertise. I was so impressed by everyone, wishing I had something to share too. A man in my dream spoke two words to me: *kingdom finances*. When I awoke, God gave me a download of the structure for this book and the concept of kingdom generosity.

This is more than financial freedom. It's not just about tithing, and it's certainly not just about money. It's not a prosperity gospel message, and I'm not here to convince you to give more to the church.

Kingdom generosity is a way of life rooted in open-handed living. It's the result of an overflowing heart fully surrendered to Jesus with the desire to see His kingdom come. It's a call to live for eternity and to fix our gaze heavenward. More than just how we handle money, kingdom generosity influences how we utilize our time, talents, and treasures. It's not simply a one-time action but rather a lifestyle firmly built upon the foundation of Christ that allows us to experience the abundant life Jesus describes in John 10:10.

For those struggling with scarcity, kingdom generosity provides the way to provision. For those burdened with financial stress and worry, kingdom generosity provides the blueprint to release. For those wavering in trusting God as their ultimate provider, kingdom generosity exposes the lies and replaces them with truth. For those wrestling with control, kingdom generosity provides the path to surrender—a losing of oneself that brings a level of abundance that could never be achieved on our own. For those wondering how to steward wealth well, kingdom generosity provides the clarity you're looking for.

You were never meant to live clenched and afraid, uncertain, worried, and stressed. If that describes you, know this: you're not broken, and you're not alone. You're being invited into something deeper. God is calling His people to live wildly generous and radically free—not just with their money but with their whole lives. You don't have to have all the answers. God isn't looking for perfection. He just wants your heart.

How can you live out this lifestyle? And, more importantly, how can you break free from the financial fear, control, doubts, stress, or worries that plague the world today? The path to kingdom generosity is a journey. It's filled with daily surrender, incremental growth and progress in obedience to our Lord and Savior, and ever-increasing joy as we receive the outpouring of God's goodness in our lives. Just like a seed that is planted requires daily care and attention, the seed of kingdom generosity, once planted in your life, slowly grows until you one day examine the reflection and see a tree providing a canopy of protection and shade to those who are lost, broken, and hurting.

In this book, I share how every person can walk in radical devotion to God through their time, talents, and treasures to live an eternally-minded life of abundance. You'll discover how to break free from the lie of scarcity, give in faith no matter your circumstances, and walk in true stewardship. You'll see how your generosity moves the heart of God, how to fight the battle of giving from a place of victory, and how generosity brings the kingdom to earth while shaping your legacy. Most of all, you'll learn how to step into the abundant life Jesus promised while living generously in ways that shape eternity.

My prayer is that this book inspires you to love Jesus passionately, live for Jesus fully, walk with Jesus regularly, and obey His voice fearlessly. May we live to see a pure and spotless bride worthy of the reward of His suffering.

1

SURRENDERING YOUR WALLET

Create in me a clean heart, O God; and renew a
right spirit within me.

PSALM 51:10 KJV

Maybe you grabbed this book because you're living paycheck to paycheck, worried about how you'll pay your bills, and stressed because finances seem to be out of control. Bills are racking up, your financial future is daunting, and it seems like you'll never be able to get ahead. Or maybe you're on the opposite end of the spectrum; your financial future is solid. You have enough to get by, maybe even plenty, but somehow still feel like you're missing something. You believe in Jesus and sometimes even give to the church, but if you're honest, giving feels more like an obligation than a joy, a religious exercise instead of a liberating act. Perhaps you're somewhere in the middle, so caught up in the fast pace of life that you've hardly had a chance to pause and ask yourself, "Is there more to life than chasing whatever comes next?"

I believe we are about to witness a move of God that will shake the earth. God is waking up His church to live radical lives of abundance *through* their generosity. Generosity is the spark that ignites the flame of the abundant life Jesus describes in John 10:10.

Through our simple obedience and acts of generosity, God can take our life from mundane and predictable to a wild adventure. And it only requires a simple yes. A yes to step into whatever God has in store for your life. A yes to surrendering control of your wallet, entrusting it to the One who provided the finances in the first place.

More than self-help or willpower, this is exactly the opposite. Full surrender is the only path to experiencing full freedom. It's about breaking off forever the financial fears, doubts, worries, and stress that plague so many of us—living life never worried about your bank account, paycheck, or provision because you fully trust your heavenly Father to provide.

This is the type of life where, when the world tells you to store up, save, and plan for the worst, you run in the opposite direction. You look for ways to bless others, encourage, build up, and share freely—ways to give without needing to receive anything in return because what you've already received is far more valuable than anything anyone could ever offer. This life is one hundred percent secure, but not through your own means. This is where your identity, purpose, and calling blend together to impact neighborhoods to nations. This life is the kind you read about in the book of Acts.

So much more than a message about tithing or budgeting, and the opposite of a prosperity gospel, this is real transformation of the heart and a paradigm shift in our mind. You were never meant to live fearful and afraid. You were created to be different from the world. You were meant to be a tree firmly planted, unmovable, and unshakeable despite whatever comes your way. When the storms of life, winds of change, droughts of famine, and rains of breakthrough come, you can continue to stand firm and grow.

God wants to invite you on this adventure. An adventure where your life is maximized for kingdom impact. A life where you witness the goodness of God and His blessings in your life daily. This type of life is available to anyone who wants it. In fact, Jesus promised it. But the way into it is completely counterintuitive. It requires full surrender.

SOMETIMES FAITH LOOKS FOOLISH

Was I ready to give up everything to follow Jesus, *including my finances?* I was in a small chapel at Faith Bible College in Tauranga, New Zealand, when a girl from Canada took the stage, announcing she was selling her car back home to pay for her mission trip and for a few others there. I couldn't believe it. I thought it was the dumbest thing I had ever heard—so impractical—and I was sure she would soon regret it.

Though I knew Jesus and believed in His power, my heart was cluttered with doubt, skepticism, and the false belief that God alone was not enough. Sure, God could do anything, but He also gave us a brain we should use, talents that were ours, and treasures (money) that we earned. I sat back witnessing the scene, ready to learn from her mistake and make sure I never acted so foolishly. Boy, was I wrong!

I was part of a group called Youth With A Mission (YWAM) and found myself in New Zealand after God impressed on my heart to go on a missions trip, supernaturally providing for me to be there. A couple of months prior, I was sitting in the back row of an evening finance class while finishing my master's degree in business administration. I sensed the Lord directing my heart to go, but I didn't know where, and, even if I did, I didn't want to go. While sitting in the very back row of the lecture, I opened my computer browser and stumbled upon a YWAM base offering a tuition-free school. I was intrigued but still hesitant to pause my life and go. A roundtrip plane ticket alone cost $1,400 from Los Angeles to New Zealand.

I was conflicted, internally feeling one way, externally feeling another, fighting with my own thoughts of doing what was rational versus what I felt like God said. The next day, I looked through the mail only to find a reimbursement check for my college tuition in the amount of $1,400—the exact price of the plane ticket. With this confirmation, I took it as a sign of God's speaking and signed up for the school, booking my flight to leave in January once the semester concluded.

It was with this background that I found myself at the Faith Bible College chapel listening to this girl profess that she was selling her possessions. Surprisingly, it wasn't just this girl who was selling possessions and leaving things behind to follow Jesus to the mission field; there were others too. Some were selling the little they had or stepping out in faith, believing God was calling them even though they didn't have the funds to provide for their needs. I couldn't believe how reckless and unprepared this group of people was—how poorly they were stewarding money and how unwise they had been to get to that point. Why would someone act so foolish? Didn't they understand that God should be revered, not forced to provide? Yet somehow, over the next few weeks, I watched God provide day after day for unmet needs. Random donations, small and large, trickled in. Daily, there were new stories of God's provision, enabling those who wanted to participate in the Lord's commission to do so.

During that season, I learned a new aspect of God's provision and witnessed kingdom generosity in action. The simple truth was one that girl from Canada already knew: with a fully surrendered heart for Jesus, you will always have more than enough. This was a simple but powerful truth yet to take root in my heart but one that sparked my personal journey. I was saved, yes, but I had not yet experienced the abundant life where kingdom generosity thrives.

LIFE AS A BELIEVER

There are three pivotal moments in the life of a believer, which are beautifully illustrated through the Old Testament: when the

Israelites were brought out of Egypt, when they crossed the Red Sea, and when they passed through the Jordan River.

The exodus from Egypt and the protection from the angel of death by the blood of the lamb on the doorposts symbolize salvation from sin. This marks the first phase of the life of the believer when we come to realize that we are sinners in need of a Savior. Jesus' blood on the cross saves us from sin.

> For all have sinned and fall short of the glory of God. (Romans 3:23)

> For the wages of sin is death, but the gift of God is eternal life in Christ Jesus our Lord. (Romans 6:23)

> For God so loved the world that he gave his one and only Son, that whoever believes in him shall not perish but have eternal life. (John 3:16)

Through this heroic act from our Savior, we are forever freed from the penalty of death, entering into a new life with Christ. From that moment on, we are guaranteed a place in heaven and begin the life of sanctification.

The crossing of the Red Sea represents baptism, whereby Christians, once saved, openly profess and make a public demonstration of their love for Christ.

> Therefore go and make disciples of all nations, baptizing them in the name of the Father and of the Son and of the Holy Spirit. (Matthew 28:19)

> *Whoever believes and is baptized will be saved, but whoever does not believe will be condemned.* (Mark 16:16)

> Peter replied, "Repent and be baptized, every one of you, in the

name of Jesus Christ for the forgiveness of your sins. And you will receive the gift of the Holy Spirit." (Acts 2:38)

I believed in Jesus at an early age, asked Him into my heart, and was baptized around the age of four. I knew I was saved, but I had no idea there was more to life with Christ. I thought life was about doing your best to follow the rules, read your Bible, and pray. I lacked a fresh revelation of God's goodness, understanding of His provision, and clarity of His plans and how He wanted to use me as a vessel for bringing His kingdom to earth. It wasn't until I witnessed kingdom generosity in Faith Bible College's chapel that I began to realize there was more—an abundant life—but the way to get there was countercultural.

Upon leaving Egypt (salvation) and crossing the Red Sea (baptism), the Israelites didn't enter the promised land until they passed through the Jordan River. This final crossing of water represents our baptism in the Spirit, whereby we enter into the promises of new life. Once we receive Jesus, we receive the Spirit, evidenced as Paul writes in Ephesians 1:13: "When you believed, you were marked in him with a seal, the promised Holy Spirit."

The Holy Spirit is a deposit—like an engagement ring—signifying our salvation to come (Ephesians 1:14). Scripture clearly points to the importance of this third baptism. John the Baptist spoke of it in Matthew, Jesus Himself testified to this new birth later in John, and Paul shares it in Acts.

I baptize you with water for repentance. But after me comes one who is more powerful than I, whose sandals I am not worthy to carry. He will baptize you with the Holy Spirit and fire. (Matthew 3:11)

Jesus answered, "Very truly I tell you, no one can enter the kingdom of God unless they are born of water and the Spirit." (John 3:5)

While Apollos was at Corinth, Paul took the road through the interior and arrived at Ephesus. There he found some disciples and asked them, "Did you receive the Holy Spirit when you believed?" They answered, "No, we have not even heard that there is a Holy Spirit." So Paul asked, "Then what baptism did you receive?" "John's baptism," they replied. Paul said, "John's baptism was a baptism of repentance. He told the people to believe in the one coming after him, that is, in Jesus." On hearing this, they were baptized in the name of the Lord Jesus. When Paul placed his hands on them, the Holy Spirit came on them, and they spoke in tongues and prophesied. (Acts 19:1-6)

While the Israelites were saved from death (salvation) and washed of sin as a sign of repentance through the crossing of the Red Sea (baptism), it was not until they passed through the Jordan River that they inherited the blessings promised to their forefather, Abraham—the abundant life of the promised land. We see this promise made back in Genesis 12:7 finally fulfilled: "To your offspring I will give this land."

What is the abundant life? Jesus explains in John 10:10 (NKJV): "The thief does not come except to steal, and to kill, and to destroy. I have come that they may have life, and that they may have *it* more abundantly." The abundant life is a lifestyle that takes hold of the promises of God and fully inherits His blessings. It's the fullest life possible with Christ as leader. But here's the catch: The abundant life isn't one to be possessed, and it can't be achieved. It's simply received. And we can only receive this life through surrender.

BREAKING OFF FEAR, CONTROL, AND THE LIE OF SCARCITY

All too often, we put God in a box. What I mean is that we add God to our neatly packed collection of life that we compartmentalize in different boxes. We have our religion box (where God lives), which we check off on Sundays. We have our work box, which we devote our time to during the week. We have our friend box. Our family box. Our sport or leisurely activity box. Our hobby box. We put God in a box and then organize our lives in such a way that each box corresponds to a day of the week, allowing us to forecast, plan, and arrange our schedules accordingly. That was me. Saved at an early age, grew up in church and attended a Christian school, yet still missing out on the abundant life Jesus promised.

What held me back is the same thing I believe holds many of us back still today—the lie of scarcity. The belief that God alone is not enough and He needs my help. The problem with this belief system is that I am in charge. I am in control, and Jesus is my follower. I dictate the direction of my life and kindly ask God to bless me on the way. I don't actively seek Him, and I certainly don't follow Him. I merely prayed a prayer of salvation and continued on my way. I was missing *transformation*—true heart change coming from the place of surrender. For me, it was the lie of scarcity. Theologically, I knew God would provide in theory, but I didn't believe that applied to me, and I didn't believe God would come and meet me in my situation.

Maybe you are in the same place I was. Maybe it's not control or the lie of scarcity but the lie that you don't have enough. It's the idea that once you make more—once you get that promotion, buy the house, or accomplish whatever is next—then you'll fully surrender your heart to Jesus. Maybe you doubt God like I did. You doubt that He would do the same for you that you've seen Him do in the Bible or for others in your life. Perhaps it's simply that you don't need God. Your life is so busy, and you're so self-sufficient, that there isn't any space for God in the car you're driving—if He's even in the back seat at all.

These fears, doubts, worries, anxieties, and desire for control weigh us down. They hold us back from experiencing the abundant life. Here's the reality: the abundant life is only fully activated through our generosity! We can't experience the fullness of what God has in store by holding back. It's only through complete, total surrender and open-handed living that we begin to walk in the abundance. The lifestyle of kingdom generosity is a means by which we grow in our relationship with Jesus, our intimacy with Him, where we stretch our faith and rest in His blessings and goodness. We must break off the fear, doubt, and worries holding us back so we may take hold of something better. We must understand God's goodness, His plans and purposes for our life, and our heavenly calling so that, through this knowledge, we can walk a generous life and live fulfilled.

WHEN I JUMPED ALL IN

About six months after I returned home from YWAM, I was looking for a job. It was 2013, and though the Great Recession of 2008 had passed, it was still not a strong job market. I applied everywhere and could not find a job. Finally, I landed an internship, cold-calling small business owners to set up meetings for senior sales representatives. It was three days a week, and I spent six hours a day on the phone facing constant rejection. I wasn't good at it and didn't like it. I was stressed but persevered, eventually being offered a full-time role after the summer.

I was four weeks into the job, smack in the middle of new-hire training, when I had an encounter with the Lord I will never forget. I woke up from a dream with Luke 18:22 on my heart. I expected something encouraging. I had never experienced God through a dream or known so tangibly that He was speaking to me. Excitedly, I opened my Bible and looked up the verse.

> When Jesus heard this, he said to him, "You still lack one thing. Sell everything you have and give to the poor, and you will have treasure in heaven. Then come, follow me."

What!? I couldn't believe it. I was on fire for Jesus after YWAM. I loved evangelizing and wanted to become a full-time missionary. I didn't know what to do. I thought I did everything right. My heart was fully surrendered (or so I thought), but it turns out my wallet was not.

The Lord wanted my full heart—including my finances—but I didn't know if I could give it. Could I truly trust God with my finances and live completely open-handed? I wrestled with this question for a few days. Looking back, I realize it was God's personal invitation to me into a lifestyle of kingdom generosity.

After much prayer and consideration, I concluded that there was no one better to lead my life than Jesus, the One who understands my intrinsic wants and desires better than anyone. I decided to go all in. Malachi 3:10 gave me hope: "'Bring the whole tithe into the storehouse, that there may be food in my house. Test me in this,' says the Lord Almighty, 'and see if I will not throw open the floodgates of heaven and pour out so much blessing that there will not be room enough to store it.'"

This would be my test. If God didn't keep His word, I'd write Him off as a liar and be off the hook to live for Him. What blows me away about Malachi 3:10 is that this is the only verse where God invites us to test Him—to show Himself faithful through His Word on our behalf, specifically regarding our finances. It's a wildly radical concept.

I withdrew $500 (all I had in my bank account), put it in an envelope, and placed it in my neighbor's mailbox across the street. I recently learned that, due to a cancer diagnosis, he was no longer able to work. I then drove to work and quit my job. I knew I had been faithful, and I was excited to see what God planned next.

For a few weeks, nothing happened. I was unemployed, broke, and living at home with my parents. With no job and an uncertain future, I began a three-month season of wandering, debating what I should do next for a career. I wanted to be a full-time missionary or teacher, but the Lord continually spoke to my heart about going into business.

I searched everywhere for a job. I was overly qualified for many positions but still had no luck. I even applied for a job selling satellite television subscriptions at Walmart and Costco, where I knew the team lead, and was still rejected.

I eventually landed a job selling insurance. But, before I could begin, I needed to pass a state exam to receive my insurance license. As I studied for the exam, I realized I already passed the more important test: surrendering my wallet.

Over the next decade, my journey into kingdom generosity has taken me from zero in my bank account to abundance. From fear, stress, and worry over finances to complete surrender and trust. From longing for more and striving for the next job or promotion to rest and peace. From struggles with impostor syndrome to certainty in my purpose and calling. From giving out of religious obligation to joyful, Spirit-led giving.

I have seen the blessings of God across my life in little moments and in the significant ones. I have seen so much evidence of God's goodness through a lifestyle of kingdom generosity that I know it to be true. I know for certain that what He has done in my life is available for you too. God wants to take you on a journey into kingdom generosity with Him. It's the most amazing, wonderful, life-giving experience I've known—and it's available to you today. Are you ready to say yes?

2

WHAT'S IN YOUR HAND?

*But Samuel replied: "Does the LORD delight in
burnt offerings and sacrifices as much as in
obeying the LORD? To obey is better than sacrifice, and to heed is better than the fat of rams."*

1 SAMUEL 15:22

Once we say yes to Jesus and choose to fully surrender, a life of kingdom generosity is surprisingly quite simple. Jesus confirms this in Matthew 11:30, "For my yoke is easy and my burden is light." One of my favorite pieces of advice came from my father-in-law, who said, "I remind myself that things of God are simple." That statement perfectly captures the essence of Matthew 11:30. Our journey to the abundant life isn't meant to be difficult. It's not meant to be a struggle, fight, or huge effort. It's meant to be easy. It simply requires saying a continual yes to God.

We have a tendency to overcomplicate the gospel and insert our own efforts in place of God. How often have we held ourselves back because we didn't feel qualified, capable—like we had enough—or ready? God isn't waiting for us to get up to His level before He will use us; He meets us *where* we are and elevates us *through* Him. For me, it was a simple yes that I would get a job in business and work that to the fullest of my ability.

As we look at the world around us, it's easy to get caught up in the rat race of life. Land the job, buy the car, marry the spouse, save the money, take the trip, save for this or that, and all the while lose sight of the true purpose of life. We were meant to reflect Christ and help others see Him. That's it! That's our only task, and the way to get started is simple: look at what's currently in your hands.

The Old Testament tells us in Ecclesiastes 9:10, "Whatever your hand finds to do, do it with all your might." Or, said a different way in Colossians 3:23, "Whatever you do, work at it with all your heart, as working for the Lord, not for human masters."

God uses whatever is in your hands. When we look at Scripture, we regularly see God meets people where they are and uses what they have to work for His plan. And here's the best part: as followers of Jesus, we are already enriched in every way for this kingdom purpose. 1 Corinthians 1:5 tells us, "For in him you have been enriched in every way—with all kinds of speech and with all knowledge." How I love that! Not only do we already have something in our hands, but God has already enriched it.

Looking at Moses, we see God took the staff he held and enriched it to free a people from generational slavery. When we look at David, we see God used his harp and enriched it to inspire billions with his psalms. Nehemiah's cup was the very tool God used to win favor with King Artaxerxes and bring the Israelites out of exile. Once used for fish, God enriched Peter's nets to teach him how to fish for people. The list goes on and on. This isn't just something God has done in the past; He's still doing it today.

Maybe you're a teacher and have an opportunity to mentor kids through an after-school Bible club. Maybe you're a talented musician and can write music that honors Him. Maybe you're a plumber and can offer your skill set to help friends and those in need on weekends like my friend Tim does. Maybe you're a businessperson and can be a positive mentor to a colleague. Whatever your situation, we all have something to offer, a part to play, and a kingdom purpose to live out.

While God starts with whatever is in our hands, He doesn't stop there. Every area of our life becomes more beautiful, more holy, more flourishing, and more impactful as we pursue our relationship with Jesus. Our vocational callings as teachers, plumbers, or businesspeople improve as we step into this calling. Here's the exciting part: slowly and surely, over time, our speech and knowledge also change. We begin to reflect our King.

DO YOU HEAR HIM?

Nothing has changed my relationship with Jesus more than learning how to hear His voice. Hearing His voice has been like injecting rocket fuel into my life of faith. God desires to have a relationship with His children. From the beginning of creation, we see God's desire for communion in the cool of the day with Adam and Eve (Genesis 3:8-10). Throughout the Bible, we see evidence of God speaking to His people. Jesus declares, "My sheep hear my voice" (John 10:27 ESV). There is a powerful transformation in our lives as we go from the abstract belief that God speaks to the personal revelation that God *will* speak to *me*. God wants to speak to *you* about your situation—your cares, worries, concerns, and joys. It's not something reserved for the hyper-holy or pastors, but for everyone. The Bible illustrates a myriad of ways God speaks: from dreams, visions, or the Bible (Word of God); through creation, angels, signs, and wonders; or, the most common, a still small voice.

There is no shortage of desire on God's end to speak. Often, the holdup is our ability to listen. We have the volume of this physical world and our busy lives so high we miss the opportunity to hear the still small voice. Our distractions get in the way of the daily communion the Father wants to have with his kids. If I, being earthly, want to have a relationship with my son and speak to him, how much more does our good Father in heaven (Matthew 7:11)? The psalmist shares how vast God's thoughts are toward him in Psalm 139:17-18.

> How precious to me are your thoughts, God! How vast is the sum of them! Were I to count them, they would outnumber the grains of sand—when I awake, I am still with you.

God's thoughts are vast indeed toward us, so much so that He even knows the number of hairs on our heads (Luke 12:7). Once I understood that God's speaking wasn't a spooky, hyper-spiritual experience, my eyes opened to the spiritual. With new eyes of faith, we can open our hearts to Jesus to receive from Him. For me, it looks like simply saying, "God, I know that you speak; please remove anything that prevents me from hearing you. I invite you to speak. What do you want to say to me?"

That's it! And then, I wait and see what comes into my mind. I mix faith with the Word: faith that God hears our prayers and trust in the Word of God, which says His sheep hear His voice. It's a practical but powerful exercise. God usually responds with a still small voice. The best way to describe it is as a pervasive thought or feeling outside your normal thought life. For me, the way I check if I'm hearing from God is a quick gauge of three points.

1. Is this thought outside of my normal day-to-day habits?
2. Does this thought align with the Bible?
3. Is this thought for good (James 1:17)?

Following this quick process, I can identify the voice of God in my life. I'll share a simple, real example. Have you ever been praying when a random person suddenly comes to mind? You may not have spoken with them for a while, but you start thinking about that person. You wonder how they are doing. This may be the voice of God. We can lean into this voice and not just pray for that person but ask God what He would like us to say to encourage them. Many times, I have followed this prompting and sent a simple text message. You wouldn't believe the power of a small, timely encouragement when connected to the voice of God. When we hear God's voice, we supercharge our faith and partner with Him in bringing heaven to earth. I encourage you to take time to pray, expectant to hear from the God of creation. He wants to speak and reveal Himself to you afresh.

The Bible says we should enter His gates with thanksgiving and His courts with praise (Psalm 100:4). Create space for God to speak, even now. Turn on some worship music. Begin to thank God for what He has done and is doing in your life. What are you grateful for? How has He blessed you recently? Thank Him for that. Praise Him for His goodness. For His holiness, kindness, faithfulness, and gentleness. As you open yourself up to Him, you'll be amazed at what He says.

DON'T DESPISE THE SMALL BEGINNINGS

My heart transformation began shortly after I started working and offered up what was in my hands. Though my first job with a master's degree paid $15 per hour, I had a renewed vision and purpose knowing that God was using what was in my hands. My calling into the business world became clear. It was obvious to me that God wanted to use my vocation, though I didn't know why. I felt like the Lord was sharing that though my passion was for missions, He was using my calling in business to fund the mission field. God was making me a financier for His kingdom.

Though I selfishly wanted to be on the front lines, He was asking me to be the office funding His great commission. He was using my heart's passion in a way that would most glorify His name and align with His plans and purposes. Despite making little, God gently reminded me of Zechariah. After returning to Jerusalem from Babylonian captivity, the Israelites painstakingly worked to rebuild Solomon's Temple. During the project, the

Lord encouraged Zerubbabel through the prophet Zechariah: "'Do not despise these small beginnings, for the LORD rejoices to see the work begin, to see the plumb line in Zerubbabel's hand'" (Zechariah 4:10 NLT)

Even though my paycheck was small, I made an effort to be generous wherever I could. If anyone asked for money or time, I gave it. God encouraged me to surrender what I had—regardless of the size. During that season, I saw God promote me, advance my career, and provide in numerous ways. He gave me a free company car that included gas and car washes. He grew my salary exponentially. He moved me out of a job that was difficult and brought me into something I enjoyed. He moved me physically from Southern California to Seattle. And He tested me along the way.

After receiving a large breakthrough and landing a new job, God once again asked me to empty my bank account. I knew this was another test to check my heart as God grew my finances—to see if He was still the sole occupant. He was, and this time, it didn't feel like a test but rather an opportunity. Jesus was my source and my focus. I knew how to recognize His voice, and this time, it was easy for me to obey. I cheerfully looked for ways to give away my entire signing bonus and savings. My growing life of generosity blossomed.

What that period of life solidified in me was an open-handed lifestyle. Whatever I found in my hands, I used to glorify Jesus. This pattern sticks with me to this day. My hands are open to serve my King, and my life is set apart for God's purposes and not my own.

WHAT ARE YOU HOLDING ONTO?

As we say yes to Jesus and fully surrender our hearts to Him, we should continually identify what's in our hands that can be used for His kingdom purpose. As we direct our hearts toward Him, we may find that some things in our hands no longer have purpose and must be released.

Old habits, possessions, or even comforts must be let go at times to make space in our hearts for the new life we are entering. The good news is that God doesn't leave us worse off than before; He always ushers us into something greater.

If we look at the previous examples from the Bible of how God used what was already in a person's hand, we see evidence of this transformation. God used Moses' staff but removed his identity as a shepherd, giving him a new purpose as a leader of a nation. God used David's harp but removed him from the palace before returning him as king. God used Nehemiah's cup but removed him from the presence of the king before returning him to Israel to rebuild the temple for the King of Kings. God removed Peter from the lake before inviting him to walk on the water.

In my life, God asked me to surrender my finances before filling my hands with funds to use for His kingdom. For you, maybe it's something different. What does God need to remove from your life before fully ushering you into your new transformed identity? What thing are you holding onto that God is asking you to release? I pray that we would be a people who joyfully release our own plans and purposes in order to make space for the kingdom calling God has on our lives.

3

LIVING BY FAITH

For we walk by faith, not by sight.

2 CORINTHIANS 5:7 NKJV

Faith is the currency of the kingdom and the essential ingredient to living a lifestyle of kingdom generosity. It takes faith to leave behind our old identities, those things that once satisfied, and those habits, passions, dreams, and desires as we begin to be filled with new passions, desires, and dreams that come from the Father.

Letting go of what we hold is hard. It's comfortable, familiar, and known. It may not always be bad, but it's usually not what is best. When we open our hands for God to fill them, we are the beneficiary of an uneven trade of monumental proportions. We show up with open hearts and open hands, releasing control of what we used to possess, allowing our Savior to fill us from His treasury. More than money, God's treasury draws from the wealth of resources across the physical and the spiritual realms.

As we begin to understand the reality of the spiritual, we become more equipped to exercise our faith. Like a muscle, faith requires stretching and strengthening. When I go to the gym, I lift weights to force my muscles to respond with more muscle mass.

Though heavy and difficult in the moment, I know that post-workout, my body will be stronger and my overall health will be better. Similarly, as we exercise our faith, it strengthens over time. When we look back, what once looked challenging, impossible, stressful, or fearful, one day becomes manageable or even easy. The second time God asked me to empty my bank account was much easier, not because what He asked was any different but because my faith grew.

There's not a singular moment that we can point back to and say, "That's when I received faith." It's not a specific church event, encounter, or Sunday sermon, but rather it's a gradual fellowship with Jesus that slowly but surely over time grows our faith. Just as regular weight training slowly but surely transforms your physical body so that one day you notice a difference, faith follows a similar journey. But the good news is there are ways to accelerate this journey.

In weight training, you can increase your protein intake to accelerate muscle development and position your body to recover faster. So it is with the lifestyle of kingdom generosity. There are spiritual accelerators such as prayer, fasting, and tithing. However, perhaps the most foundational accelerator to our life of kingdom generosity comes through our understanding of God's kingdom and aligning our belief system with it.

SPIRITUAL LAWS

My friend has a podcast called *The Manly Catholic*. (I'm not Catholic, but he is, and he asked me to give it a listen.) During a long drive to the airport, I listened to an episode with a guest, Jesse Romero, who shared a startling truth I never considered. He said, "In God's kingdom, God has written spiritual laws that act exactly the same in the spiritual realm as our physical laws do in the natural realm."

We are all familiar with the physical laws of the universe, regardless of whether we hold a degree in applied physics or have never attended a day of school in our lives. We know how the law of gravity pulls things down, meaning that objects fall if dropped. We understand Newton's Laws of Motion, such as "objects at rest stay at rest" (First Law) or "for every action, there is an equal and opposite reaction" (Third Law). We understand the laws of optics (how light interacts with matter), mechanics, thermodynamics (don't touch something hot), and even colloquially refer to the laws of attraction. We understand laws of physics, how atoms are held together, and many other scientific laws.

However, equally—if not more—important, there are spiritual laws governing the spiritual realm. Many of us may not be as familiar with spiritual laws as we are with physical laws. Just as you can teach basic laws of thermodynamics to a first grader and equally complex ones to a PhD student, laws are grasped at varying levels.

As I began leaning into the spiritual and living by faith, God took me on a journey that led me from where I grew up with all my friends and family in California to Washington. While living in Seattle, I had a roommate named John. He had a PhD in aerospace engineering and was the director of space for a startup rocket company. As an aside, director of space might possibly be the coolest title ever granted. Regardless of whether you possess a PhD in aerospace engineering and are responsible for ensuring rockets reach their intended targets (like John) or simply know that rockets are cool and somehow fly (like me), we all understand that there are forces of nature at play. Some of us, through our jobs or occupations, have become more familiar with these physical forces in our daily lives.

Just as some of us encounter these physical forces regularly through our work or studies, others may be more familiar with the spiritual principles shaping the spiritual realm. Paul hints at this in his letter to the Corinthians: "I gave you milk, not solid food, for you were not yet ready for it. Indeed, you are still not ready" (1 Corinthians 3:2). Even Jesus, when standing trial before Pontius Pilate, touched on this when He said, "My kingdom is not of this world" (John 18:36). Romans 8:2 says that "through Christ Jesus the law of the Spirit who gives life has set you free from the law of sin and death."

Not only is there another realm—the spiritual realm—but the spirit and the physical are often in conflict. Paul explains this in Galatians 5:17: "For the flesh desires what is contrary to the Spirit, and the Spirit what is contrary to the flesh. They are in conflict with each other, so that you are not to do whatever you want." We understand that there is a physical, fleshly, carnal appetite that desires things opposed to the spirit, and the spirit desires what opposes the flesh (physical).

Upon our salvation, we are given the Holy Spirit, our Comforter, who indwells us as believers and reveals Jesus to our hearts. One of the roles of the Comforter is to teach us and remind us of what Jesus said.

> And I will ask the Father, and he will give you another advocate to help you and be with you forever—the Spirit of truth. The world cannot accept him, because it neither sees him nor knows him. But you know him, for he lives with you and will be in you... But the Advocate, the Holy Spirit, whom the Father will send in my name, will teach you all things and will remind you of everything I have said to you. (John 14:16-17, 26)

Just as a PhD student's understanding of thermodynamics surpasses that of a third grader, we, too, can grow in our understanding of the spiritual realm as we mature in our faith and relationship with God. Understanding thermodynamics is a continuous journey of learning, always discovering new depths of knowledge—a student of this never fully comprehends the entire physical world. Likewise, our life of kingdom generosity is one of continuous discovery and growth.

If we are to live by faith, we must understand how to live by the Spirit. While the physical laws of the universe shape our reality, the deeper, often paradoxical truths that Jesus taught about the kingdom of God shape eternity. These truths can only be learned through faith. Though they may seem unstable, they are the very foundation of our life in Christ. As we build upon this foundation, letting go of the physical and clinging to the spiritual, we grow in generosity and trust. We experience freedom. Jesus fully embodied these truths and provided an example of a life lived fully by faith during His time on earth. What we see from Him is not a life centered on the pursuit of power, wealth, or self-preservation but on surrender, humility, and faith.

A PARADOXICAL KINGDOM

As Jesus taught, He often used parables to reveal spiritual realities. Some of these truths are simple to grasp, while others remain a mystery. His words and actions offer us a glimpse into a life of faith and the paradoxical nature of living by the Spirit. By exploring these paradoxes, we deepen our understanding of the spiritual life and allow them to reshape our focus.

PERHAPS FOREMOST OF these paradoxes is the idea that *in order to lead, you must serve.*

> When he had finished washing their feet, he put on his clothes and returned to his place. "Do you understand what I have done for you?" he asked them. "You call me 'Teacher' and 'Lord,' and rightly so, for that is what I am. Now that I, your Lord and Teacher, have washed your feet, you also should wash one another's feet. I have set you an example that you should do as I have done for you. Very truly I tell you, no servant is greater than his master, nor is a messenger greater than the one who sent him. Now that you know these things, you will be blessed if you do them." (John 13:12-17)

In Mark 9:35, Jesus further illustrates this point: "Anyone

who wants to be first must be the very last, and the servant of all." This is something we can apply in every area of our lives, understanding that serving others is an opportunity to be like Him.

In my career, I have made it a point to take Colossians 3:23-24 to heart:

> Whatever you do, work at it with all your heart, as working for the Lord, not for human masters, since you know that you will receive an inheritance from the Lord as a reward. It is the Lord Christ you are serving.

I literally try to imagine, if Jesus were my manager, how I would spend my day. I think of how I can help make Him look good, how I can make His job easier, how I can be a good team player, how I can deliver everything He asks of me excellently, and how I can maximize His return on my investment. It has radically transformed the way I view work and day-to-day life.

ANOTHER PARADOXICAL TRUTH is that *in order to receive, we must give.*

> Give, and it will be given to you. A good measure, pressed down, shaken together and running over, will be poured into your lap. For with the measure you use, it will be measured to you. (Luke 6:38)

It's amazing how when I give—even if it's a word of encouragement to a friend—I often find that someone later reaches out to encourage me. When I give financially, I am met with unexpected blessings. My wife and I recently gave a sum of money to a charitable cause, and the very next week our car's transmission failed. It turned out to be under warranty, so now we're receiving a $7,500 repair essentially free—a brand-new car under the hood.

That same week, our mortgage provider informed us that we had an escrow surplus—as a result, we were mailed a substantial refund check. We received back from God more than we had given.

ANOTHER EXAMPLE of this upside-down nature of the kingdom Jesus described is that *in order to enter the kingdom of heaven, we must become like children.*

> And he said: "Truly I tell you, unless you change and become like little children, you will never enter the kingdom of heaven." (Matthew 18:3)

While the kingdom of heaven is the most amazing, complex, and wonderful place imaginable, we must renew our minds to become like a child to enter it. When I find myself becoming cynical or jaded, I remind myself that it's only through childlike faith and wonder that I can draw near to God's heart.

JESUS ALSO TEACHES us that *we must lose ourselves in order to truly find ourselves.*

> For whoever wants to save their life will lose it, but whoever loses their life for me will find it. (Matthew 16:25)

I've found this to be true in my own life. As I surrendered my identity to Christ, letting go of what I used to care about so passionately, God shifted my dreams and desires. I began seeking to care for the orphan by funding wells in Africa, giving generously to women rescued from trafficking, and using money intentionally to help usher in Christ's kingdom.

But Jesus doesn't stop there. He goes further to say we must die to live:

Very truly I tell you, unless a kernel of wheat falls to the ground and dies, it remains only a single seed. But if it dies, it produces many seeds. (John 12:24)

There are many times I've had to swallow my pride, let go of resentment, and choose to forgive. In doing so, I died to my natural appetites so my spiritual life could flourish.

FINALLY, Paul shares that in the kingdom of heaven, *when we are weak, we find strength.*

That is why, for Christ's sake, I delight in weaknesses, in insults, in hardships, in persecutions, in difficulties. For when I am weak, then I am strong. (2 Corinthians 12:10)

In almost every job I've had, I've struggled with imposter syndrome. I often feel unsure of what I'm doing or what steps to take. But in those moments of weakness, I've learned to ask God daily for guidance—and He always comes through. In my most recent role, God gave me a transformative idea leading to a corporate-wide initiative with incredible impact despite the ambiguity and lack of direction I initially faced.

As we meditate on these spiritual realities, we enlarge the areas of our heart that are closed to faith. With fresh eyes, let us examine Scripture and take it as reality. May we be a people willing to walk in a way counter to the world—to be misunderstood so we might truly imitate Christ, our Lord. Let us lean into the paradoxical truths of the kingdom so we can exercise our faith and become fully useful for Jesus' kingdom.

A life of kingdom generosity requires heavenly-minded believers. We must grow in our understanding of Jesus' promises and laws so we can imitate Christ in all things. By letting go, we will grow in freedom, for we ourselves own nothing but only live to please our Father in heaven. With open hands, we receive and can freely give all things, as Christ Himself gave all. We become foolish vessels that confound the wise (1 Corinthians 1:27) by understanding the greater truths that govern our purpose and existence in this life. The freedom we find when we are willing to fully walk with kingdom laws in mind leads us down a never-ceasing, ever-fruitful, fully radical, completely free life of abundance.

DEVELOPING FAITH MARKERS

When was the last time God asked you to do something you didn't want to do? Did you obey?

While growing in faith is gradual, there are signs and markers along the way we can point to as key tests or invitations from God into greater faith. On Abraham's journey, he was invited to leave his country (Genesis 12:1). On Joshua's journey, he was encouraged to be strong and courageous (Joshua 1:9). On Elijah's journey, he was asked to confront the king (1 Kings 18:1). On Jesus' journey, He was forced to bear the cross (Luke 22:42). Our own journeys of faith have similar markers.

I loved taking road trips. My friends and I would hop in the car and drive up the coast or out to the mountains. If you've ever taken a road trip, there are markers and signs on your way to show you're headed in the right direction.

One road trip I love is from Orange County to Santa Cruz. California has a beautiful coastline, and as you head north from the warm sandy beaches of Southern California and enter Northern California, the terrain changes from gentle palm trees to rugged redwoods. On the way, I would always look for two of my favorite markers to let me know I was on the right path: Big Sur and the Elephant Seal Vista Point. Both stops allow you to get out and enjoy the natural beauty of God's creation, taking in the stunning scenery and wildlife. When my friends and I arrived at one of these markers, we knew we were nearing our end destination. I may not remember all the stops and lookouts on the eight-hour journey, but these two stand out, and looking back, passing those stops were signs that we were still on the right path.

The same is true with our life of faith. Though long, winding, and, at times, monotonous, there are distinct markers God places along our path to show us we are going the right way—that we are on the correct trajectory. He did this with Abraham, Joshua, Elijah, and even Jesus, and He does this in our lives today. These challenges, or invitations into greater, are meant to push us out of our comfort zone and into the kingdom zone—the place that requires faith because the outcome is uncertain. One of these faith markers in my life came in 2016.

My friend told me about a small mission team that was going to Iraq and suggested I pray about joining them. It was during the height of ISIS' control and a terrifying time to think about traveling to the Middle East. I immediately thought, "No way!" when it was suggested I come along; however, I didn't want to give in to fear, so I took it to God to see what He had to say about it. After praying, I couldn't shake the feeling that I was supposed to go.

It was a medical mission trip with a team of doctors performing heart surgeries—yet I had zero medical training. It made no sense why I should go. Despite this, I obeyed, stepping out in faith both vocationally (not having a purpose) and practically (wondering if I would be safe). I was fearful that I could potentially lose my life given the situation we were coming into. On the flight there, I sat next to Chris, who I had just met, discussing my fears, when he shared something I'll never forget: "I died to myself and gave up my life a long time ago. I'm not about to take it back now." What an answer! I couldn't believe his boldness.

During the week-long trip, I prayed continually in the operating rooms and helped the doctors however I could. I walked the lines of people waiting to be seen by doctors, offering entertainment, hope, and encouragement. The doctors performed surgeries on a dozen children—their hearts were physically saved and lives forever transformed—and yet, even at the end of our trip, I still had zero idea why I went.

I have learned that as we step out in faith, obedience precedes understanding. The simple steps of faith in God's Word, coupled with action, unlock a radical life of freedom. We become inoculated to the fears of man, and our focus becomes solely on Jesus. When we are willing to give what we have generously—whether it's our time, energy, or love—Jesus can use it to produce a bountiful harvest.

Little did I know that my simple act of faith, despite having no clear purpose or reason to be on that trip, was preparing me for the greatest blessing of my life. That trip directly led to me meeting my wife four years later. I would never have met her if I didn't say yes to God. He invited me to step further into faith, to be generous with my time and open-handed with my life, which left me more fulfilled—spiritually then and relationally now—through the process. It's such an uneven trade looking back!

Where is God asking you to step out in faith? Is it with your time, talent, or treasure? Is He asking you to step into the local church and participate? Is He challenging you to trust Him with tithing even though you feel like you're barely getting by? Is He prompting you to start a business? Is He reminding you to send that text, forgive that person, or change your career? If God is in it, we know it will be for our good!

4

STEWARDSHIP VERSUS OWNERSHIP

For every animal of the forest is mine, and the
cattle on a thousand hills. I know every bird in
the mountains, and the insects in the fields are
mine. If I were hungry, I would not tell you, for
the world is mine, and all that is in it.

PSALM 50:10-12

God calls us to be stewards, not owners. A steward cultivates, grows, takes care of, and fosters on behalf of another, while an owner has total control. God is the owner; we are the stewards. Our time, talents, and treasures are meant to be stewarded, not owned. Our resources are to be used for kingdom impact, not material gain or increased comfort.

God owns the cattle on a thousand hills, and all resources are His. During our short time on earth, we are generously offered by God to steward that which He provides. Therein lies the key—He has already generously provided. Everything we own, all that we have, is provided by God to us. It's not earned but received. We receive from God freely all things, and in turn, through our faithfulness and trustworthiness, we are found capable of receiving more.

A steward's mentality is much different than that of an owner. As a steward, it's easy to let go of things that aren't ours in the first place. When I rent a car, I have no problem handing over the keys after my reservation ends because I know it was borrowed. I was never planning to keep the car forever; it wasn't mine to own. Just because I may have gotten comfortable in the car for a few days doesn't mean that I was meant to keep it. When I'm stewarding resources, it's easier to live open-handed.

Stewards also take extra care. My wife and I have an old Ford Escape. We take it to the beach, where it gets wet, sandy, and dirty. We park it outside, and it gets rained on. It gets dirty quickly, and I rarely wash it. It's an old car, so I don't bother spending a lot to maintain it. My dad, on the other hand, has a like-new Chevy Silverado. Sometimes, I need to borrow my dad's truck to pick up furniture or transport other heavy items. When I drive his truck, it's a big upgrade over my Ford Escape. I drive it carefully. I pay hyper-attention. I stay in the lanes, follow all laws, park it where it won't get dirty, and try and wipe my feet off before I get in the car. I take care of that truck because it's much more expensive than my own car—I'm nervous to damage it in any way! I steward it well because I know he is being generous in letting me borrow it for my needs.

Stewards are extravagant and share freely. Have you ever gone out to eat with someone else's credit card? Maybe it's a corporate card or a parent's or friend's card. When you went to leave a tip, wasn't it much easier to be generous? *Why?* Because the money wasn't yours to begin with. In high school, my friends' dad gave us $40 for pizza. With $40 in hand, we didn't order Domino's or Little Caesars—we ordered Chicago deep-dish pizza. We got the best! It's easier to be extravagant with someone else's money. We can bring the same extravagant steward mentality to our own possessions.

Maybe you're like me. Growing up, when I prayed, I made

sure to thank God for my talents. I went to church, tithed, and sometimes read the Bible and prayed when I needed something. I owned my time, and I certainly owned my treasures—the chief of which was money. It wasn't that I was particularly greedy. It was much more subtle than that. I was in control. It's a small difference but likely a worse heart condition. I controlled what I made, how I spent it, and where it was allocated. I calculated the cost of everything. Inviting friends over, I was highly aware of how much each person ate, how much the pizza I bought cost, and how "generous" I was being. Generosity was an obligation, and one I didn't particularly enjoy. I was entirely caught up in an ownership worldview. I owned the path I was on and wanted God to kindly bless me along the way.

However, the lifestyle of kingdom generosity that Jesus calls us into is not one of ownership but of stewardship. This life is simply a rental, a tryout. We are meant to steward what God provides us through our time, talents, and treasures for His kingdom purposes. Whether we are good stewards or poor stewards depends on our actions—and our actions are shaped by our perspective as an owner versus a steward. Our purpose in life is meant to align with God's purposes. Jesus illustrates this through His Parable of the Talents.

THE PARABLE OF THE TALENTS

The Parable of the Talents is well known, but it's important to consider its context. The disciples are with Jesus in Jerusalem when they ask what the signs of the end of the age will be.

> As Jesus was sitting on the Mount of Olives, the disciples came to him privately. "Tell us," they said, "when will this happen, and what will be the sign of your coming and of the end of the age?" (Matthew 24:3)

In response, Jesus explains what must soon take place and

how the kingdom of heaven—His government—will take shape. The kingdom of heaven is best defined by Jesus in Luke 17:20-21:

> The coming of the kingdom of God is not something that can be observed, nor will people say, "Here it is," or "There it is," because the kingdom of God is in your midst.

I've heard it explained that we live in an in-between space—between the kingdom that has come and the kingdom that is not yet. What this means is that Jesus' death on the cross once and for all provided a sacrifice for our sins and restored all authority to His believers. This authority was surrendered to the devil when Adam and Eve sinned. Upon that original sin, the devil usurped the authority that was intended for mankind. Jesus restored the rightful order upon His death. On the Mount of Olives, shortly before His ascension, Jesus makes this clear: "All authority in heaven and on earth has been given to me" (Matthew 28:18).

All authority now belongs to our Savior, Jesus Christ, and He empowers His believers to carry out His charge to go and make disciples, the Great Commission.

> Therefore go and make disciples of all nations, baptizing them in the name of the Father and of the Son and of the Holy Spirit, and teaching them to obey everything I have commanded you. And surely I am with you always, to the very end of the age. (Matthew 28:19-20)

We know that Jesus now has all authority, and He commissions His servants to carry out His plans on earth before the full restorative work of His divine purposes is accomplished during His reign in the millennial kingdom. This is important context to understand the type of stewardship that Jesus expects from His followers. Explaining what the kingdom of heaven will be like at the end, Jesus shares:

Again, it will be like a man going on a journey, who called his servants and entrusted his wealth to them. To one he gave five bags of gold, to another two bags, and to another one bag, each according to his ability. Then he went on his journey. The man who had received five bags of gold went at once and put his money to work and gained five bags more. So also, the one with two bags of gold gained two more. But the man who had received one bag went off, dug a hole in the ground and hid his master's money. After a long time the master of those servants returned and settled accounts with them. The man who had received five bags of gold brought the other five. "Master," he said, "you entrusted me with five bags of gold. See, I have gained five more." His master replied, "Well done, good and faithful servant! You have been faithful with a few things; I will put you in charge of many things. Come and share your master's happiness!" The man with two bags of gold also came. "Master," he said, "you entrusted me with two bags of gold; see, I have gained two more." His master replied, "Well done, good and faithful servant! You have been faithful with a few things; I will put you in charge of many things. Come and share your master's happiness!" Then the man who had received one bag of gold came. "Master," he said, "I knew that you are a hard man, harvesting where you have not sown and gathering where you have not scattered seed. So I was afraid and went out and hid your gold in the ground. See, here is what belongs to you." His master replied, "You wicked, lazy servant! So you knew that I harvest where I have not sown and gather where I have not scattered seed? Well then, you should have put my money on deposit with the bankers, so that when I returned I would have received it back with interest. So take the bag of gold from him and give it to the one who has ten bags. For whoever has will be given more, and they will have an abundance. Whoever does not have, even what they have will be taken from them. And throw that worthless servant outside, into the darkness, where there will be weeping and gnashing of teeth." (Matthew 25:14-30)

The master invests in each of the three men—not equally, but consistently and duly—according to their ability. The amount of investment is not what impresses Jesus (it came from Him anyway). The return each man gained from the investment is what mattered to Him. In a true capitalistic sense, look at the response to the first two men. Both the man who was given five bags of gold and the man who was given two bags of gold make an equal return on investment (ROI). Notice the master's response: "Well done, good and faithful servant! You have been faithful with a few things; I will put you in charge of many things." It's not the amount of return but the return on investment. Both men received equal reward and were placed in charge of *many things*. In Luke 12:48, Jesus shares a similar concept.

> But the one who does not know and does things deserving punishment will be beaten with few blows. From everyone who has been given much, much will be demanded; and from the one who has been entrusted with much, much more will be asked.

Our stewardship does not depend on the amount we are blessed with but on what we do with the blessings we receive. The faithful steward who invests wisely will be rewarded with more, while the foolish steward will be stripped of even what they had.

STEWARDING TIME, TALENTS, AND TREASURES

More than just our money, God is interested in the way we steward our time, talents, and treasures. Are we maximizing His investment in us for kingdom impact? God wants fully surrendered hearts, not partial surrender. He wants all our time, talents, and treasures. Once we understand all that we have is from Him and was received by gift, it becomes easier to operate as a steward.

Time

My grandma is ninety-one years old, and she moved into my parents' house a couple of years ago. She is widowed and suffers from dementia, which made it necessary for her to no longer live on her own. Recently, she broke her ankle and was transferred to a nursing home to recover and be tended to. The nursing home is about half an hour from where my parents live. Despite the distance, my mom makes it a priority to almost daily visit her and provide her with company and care. My mom spent her time looking after her to the best of her ability—maximizing the use of her time.

There are moments when my grandma doesn't remember her children, which makes it hard for my mom, but she lovingly sets aside her agenda to take care of her mother. I can think of no better example of truly embodying what religion looks like than in James 1:27: "Look after orphans and widows in their distress and to keep oneself from being polluted by the world."

Another example is my friend Laura. Inspired by Jesus Burgers, a ministry that passes out late-night hamburgers to students on college campuses, Laura decided to start her own version: Mac and Jesus. Laura bakes five pounds of macaroni and cheese and drives to the Newport Beach Pier to pass it out for free to anyone who stops by. There's no agenda or gimmicks; she simply passes out food.

People often ask her why she is doing this and what her motivation is, looking for the catch. Radical generosity, where nothing is expected in return, confounds the world. It doesn't compute. As she generously uses her time, questions come up, and opportunities arise to pray for people and share the love of Jesus. The stories of people receiving prayer and weeping as a result of the simple act of dedicating time to stand outside and pass out macaroni and cheese are an amazing illustration of stewarding time in a way that aligns with the heart of our Savior.

Talents

Perhaps the greatest example of stewardship I have witnessed is from the doctors who perform heart surgeries for children in Iraq that I shared in the previous chapter. Though it costs them greatly to make two trips a year—both financially and personally—their purpose is priceless. These three wonderfully faithful stewards of their vocational gifting, time, resources, money, and energy (I was exhausted after only four hours of sleep that first night, yet they awoke with purpose and clarity of vision) generously pour their all into serving an underprivileged group of children.

They do not seek accolades or the praise of men but rather look to please God. In faithful obedience, they travel to some of the most desolate, dangerous, and depressed regions of the world to provide life-saving medical care. From Kosovo to Yemen, from Mongolia to Iraq, these doctors perform physical heart surgeries as an expression of Christ's love—restoring bodies with the hope of leading souls to spiritual transformation through an encounter with the Anointed One, Jesus.

The outpouring of love expressed through these doctors' multifaceted generosity offers a blueprint for how we can steward our giftings well. Though not all of us are trained as doctors, we all can look outward to see where we can apply the talents we do have to make an eternal impact. My wife, Emma, who was a professional contemporary dancer in New York City did this well. It was always her dream to become a dancer, but more than that, her heart's desire was to dance for a Christian dance company and use her talents for kingdom impact.

After searching for a Christian dance company and finding none existed, in response to prompting from the Holy Spirit, Emma started the first one in New York City. She worked tirelessly to recruit dancers, develop choreography, find dance spaces, and schedule rehearsals, all while balancing full-time work as a dancer and side jobs to get by in the city. She put on multiple full-length shows, and her choreography was featured in festivals throughout the city, producing art intended purely to honor Jesus. Funding this entirely out of pocket, Emma was unconcerned with the financial cost. She was more focused on releasing the presence of Jesus and changing the spiritual atmosphere over a city and industry through her talents.

Finally, I'll turn to my friend Tim. I met Tim in YWAM, and we quickly became friends. Tim was raised on a dairy farm in New Zealand and is an incredibly hard worker. He loves to work with his hands and, upon coming to America, trained as a plumber. He runs around all week fixing both commercial and residential plumbing issues as they come up yet still makes time to use his skillset for the kingdom.

Whenever I've had plumbing issues, Tim is always quick to come over that weekend to "take a look" (which actually means fix it). It's not unusual for Tim to work all week and be on call during the weekend but still willingly jump in to fix problems for others. It's not just for me either. Tim offers this up to all his friends and anyone else he knows because he understands that his vocational training can have a kingdom impact by blessing others. He has literally saved people tens of thousands of dollars in plumbing work through his selfless, relentless work ethic. No matter what job or gifting we have, whether it feels significant or not, it can be redeemed with a generous mindset.

I pray we will see thousands more examples of overflowing generosity in the next generation—born from wildly generous Jesus followers.

Treasures

To most, nothing is more treasured or sacred than their home. Last year, my wife and I bought our own. We were ecstatic to have more space for our growing family—especially our little two-year-old boy. Shortly after moving in, we met our next-door neighbors, David and Bonny, who are the kindest, most humble Christian couple. They have six kids—three natural children and three adopted. After raising their first three children, David and Bonny adopted three girls from China. Pouring more than love into these girls, they opened the entirety of their material treasures to raise these girls and provide a foundation of love, support, and family.

Though I'm sure it's not easy, and by all means costly, David and Bonny aren't living for this life. They are maximizing their treasures for kingdom impact. With eyes toward heaven, they work tirelessly, daily, without accolade or recognition, to bring heaven down to earth for these three girls. As I write, I'm almost brought to tears thinking of what this unassuming couple's reception will be like upon entering the gates of heaven based on their wonderful display of kingdom generosity.

STEWARDING OUR TIME, talents, and treasures brings heaven to earth in a supernatural way. We offer what we have, and God multiplies it—expanding our generosity and increasing the impact. There is something extraordinary that happens when we bring them to the feet of Jesus. In that place, not only does heaven touch earth, but our hearts are enlarged, and we reflect our Creator. Identity and purpose collide, and through our generosity, lasting change is released.

God gives each of us unique giftings to be used for His kingdom. By adopting a steward's mentality, we begin to touch heaven with our generosity as we freely and extravagantly give and take care of all our possessions. More than money, stewarding encompasses our time, talents, and treasures, as Jesus wants each of these areas of our life to be redeemed and set aside for His kingdom's purpose.

5

GIVING AS LIFE

The wicked borrow and do not repay, but the right-eous give generously.

PSALM 37:21

Many of us are all too familiar with the rhythm of Sunday services. We show up, listen to a worship set, the announcements, a quick pitch on giving, the sermon, and a prayer, and then we close. If we're lucky, we're out the door in one hour, or so many of us feel. How backwards is that? We try to limit the presence of God to one hour on a Sunday and neglect the Author of Life. I've heard friends react to pastors bringing up money, saying it made them feel uncomfortable or that it was out of place. However, what we may not stop to ask is *what does the Bible say about money?* Many of us are familiar with the concept of a tithe, but what does a tithe actually mean? What does God require of me? Or a better question, what does God have in store for me?

Kingdom generosity is about so much more than tithing. God doesn't give us a new identity and purpose simply because He needs our money. He's not looking for royalties on our newfound callings. No, He wants to unlock something bigger, something deeper. He wants to free our hearts from burdens and bring us into joy. He wants to remove obligation and replace it with opportunity. He wants to direct us deeper into fellowship, trust, and a relationship with Him *through* our money. This is more than tithing; it's Spirit-led giving. It's giving as a means to life.

Giving as life has a powerful effect on our hearts. It is a tool that softens the most jaded of hearts and breaks a heart of stone into a heart of flesh. As Christians, we don't follow our heart; we lead it. A powerful thing happens once we begin giving: our hearts are literally transformed. Did you know that? How you spend your money has a direct correlation with your heart—the things you want most in life. How do we know this? The Bible makes it clear. Jesus lays this principle out in Matthew 6:21: "For where your treasure is, there your heart will be also." Let's read it again as if it's the first time we're encountering it. *Where your treasure is, there your heart will be also.*

If you grew up in the church like me, you are familiar with this verse. It's part of a broader passage about laying up treasures in heaven (Matthew 6:19-24).

Do not store up for yourselves treasures on earth, where moths and vermin destroy, and where thieves break in and steal. But store up for yourselves treasures in heaven, where moths and vermin do not destroy, and where thieves do not break in and steal. For where your treasure is, there your heart will be also. The eye is the lamp of the body. If your eyes are healthy, your whole body will be full of light. But if your eyes are unhealthy, your whole body will be full of darkness. If then the light within you is darkness, how great is that darkness! No one can serve two masters. Either you will hate the one and love the other, or you will be devoted to the one and despise the other. You cannot serve both God and money.

I never realized the simple practicality of the concept that your heart is where your treasure is, but it's so true. Have you ever looked at your credit card statement? I encourage you to do this. Seriously. Drop the book, pause your reading, and go check out your last month's credit card or bank statement.

Subtract the major expenses: rent, mortgage, bills, utilities, insurance, car payments, and gas. Look at what's left. What are you spending your money on? Where is your discretionary income going? Now, ask yourself, *what do you love?*

My wife and I used to get lattes quite regularly—we loved coffee! Are you a big movie buff, foodie, sports fan, traveler, partier, fashionista, or workout enthusiast? Maybe you spend a lot of money each month on sports training for your kids or on home renovation projects. Does what you love correlate to how you spend your money?

If where we spend our money is also where our heart is, how often do we unknowingly direct our hearts toward carnal activities over kingdom values? Of course, none of the things I mentioned are inherently bad, but is Jesus the priority of your life ahead of where you spend your money? Do your money habits accurately reflect your priorities?

If you feel like you're not on fire for God but are on fire with an insatiable love for something else, does that match your budget? I venture to say that where we prioritize our discretionary budget has an outsized impact on the things we truly love. Obviously, the answer isn't to stop spending money on things we enjoy, especially when many of those things are not inherently sinful or wrong. However, if there's an area of your life where you allocate money toward anything that directly opposes Scripture, I encourage you to cut it out of your budget immediately.

Ultimately, here's the real question: *Are we the ones directing our heart?* May we be the kind of people who understand the significance money plays in shaping our hearts and who actively direct our hearts into the love of Christ through how we manage our money.

GIVING AS LAW

There are many good books about the two covenants. One book that I read, which gave me a helpful foundation in differentiating the Old Testament from the New Testament, is *Destined to Reign* by Joseph Prince. He explores the distinction between the law and grace, outlining how we are freed from the law of sin and death, as Paul confidently asserts in Romans 8:2: "Because through Christ Jesus the law of the Spirit who gives life has set you free from the law of sin and death."

Among other laws in the Hebrew legal system that the Torah (the first five books of the Bible) establishes, a tithe of 10% is clearly outlined. The Torah commands Israelites to give 10% of their produce (crops, livestock, etc.) as a tithe. We see this in several passages in Leviticus and Numbers.

> A tithe of everything from the land, whether grain from the soil or fruit from the trees, belongs to the LORD; it is holy to the LORD. (Leviticus 27:30)

> The LORD said to Moses, "Speak to the Levites and say to them: 'When you receive from the Israelites the tithe I give you as your inheritance, you must present a tenth of that tithe as the LORD's offering. Your offering will be reckoned to you as grain from the threshing floor or juice from the winepress. In this way you also will present an offering to the LORD from all the tithes you receive from the Israelites. From these tithes you must give the LORD's portion to Aaron the priest. You must present as the LORD's portion the best and holiest part of everything given to you.' Say to the Levites: 'When you present the best part, it will be reckoned to you as the product of the threshing floor or the winepress. You and your households may eat the rest of it anywhere, for it is your wages for your work at the tent of meeting. By presenting the best part of it you will not be guilty in this matter; then you will not defile the holy offer-

ings of the Israelites, and you will not die.'" (Numbers 18:25-32)

In our modern, sophisticated society, we no longer trade in livestock and crops. While our currency of trade is the dollar, the principle is clear: return 10%. However, we now operate within the grace covenant Jesus established, freeing us from a place of obligation to a place of love. While 10% was required under the law, grace abounds much more! We are freed from obligation—freed to act in response to God's love. And how great is this love that we are called children of God (1 John 3:1).

While 10% may be a helpful starting point if you're like me and overtly practical, it's not the end-all. In fact, it's the starting line, not the finish line! God doesn't view a tithe as a religious exercise but as an opportunity. He isn't looking for a specific number; He wants your heart. He wants you to trust Him with your money. He wants you to experience His provision, abundance, rewards, and blessings.

A CHRISTMAS OFFERING

In December 2018, I was part of a small church in New York City of about thirty people. My friend, Chris, who had also gone on the mission trip to Iraq, attended the church when he lived in the city and told me about it after I moved to New York. To close out the year, our pastor led us into a month of generosity to coincide with Christmas. It was a small church, but our collective hunger for God was palpable and authentic. We were unified and living life together like the book of Acts. Our pastor spent the next four weeks preaching on generosity and encouraging us to lean in. He embodied generosity, as he also had a full-time job to support his family while leading the church. He was truly living generously with his time and talents.

What took place that month of December was startling. Each of us prayed about what we should give. The average age of the church was around twenty-six, and I was on the older end at twenty-nine. Outside of one married couple with two kids, I don't think anyone was over the age of thirty-five. And yet, we were a group willing to give whatever God put on our hearts. That final Sunday, seated in a small basement art studio turned church sanctuary on Sunday mornings, we watched our pastor take the stage. He was beaming as he prepared to share how much we gave leading up to Christmas. You could almost tangibly feel the spiritual gift of generosity; it was so evident.

From thirty of us, our church gave over $90,000—*ninety thousand dollars!* I was stunned. I, too, gave generously, but I wasn't expecting that. None of us were. It wasn't one large gift either. Everyone gave out of the overflow of their hearts.

That December showed me the power of what hearts fully surrendered to Jesus can do for the kingdom. A small group of twenty- to thirty-year-olds raised a special offering above our tithes of $90,000. Truly, when Jesus touches people's finances, amazing things happen.

Moving from giving as law to giving as life frees us from an indebted mentality and restores a heart posture of kingdom generosity. Our money has a powerful grip *on our* hearts. Yet, giving is a powerful tool *for our* hearts. To experience full heart transformation and the abundant life, we must not only be aware of our spending habits, but we must also actively direct our hearts through our money.

Freed from any obligation, generosity then comes from a place of overflow and awe at the goodness of God, further directing our hearts into His love. As we do so, we position ourselves to receive more freely from our Father. With unlocked hearts, we become kingdom ambassadors, leaving a wake of goodness everywhere we step. Once we bring ourselves to this place of humble submission and joyful response, we must be aware that our journey will likely be met with resistance.

6

THE BATTLE OVER GENEROSITY

And this is the testimony: God has given us eternal
life, and this life is in his Son... We know that
anyone born of God does not continue to sin; the
One who was born of God keeps them safe, and
the evil one cannot harm them. We know that
we are children of God, and that the whole
world is under the control of the evil one.

1 JOHN 5:11, 18-19

As we enter a life of kingdom generosity and begin to experience
the abundant life, we must be prepared for the inevitable opposition that will come. Generosity that makes a kingdom impact is
likely to be met with resistance as the devil begins to lose ground
through our generosity. The battle can take many forms and come
from many places, but we must stand our ground and lean on the
Word of God.

Internal battles wage war over our thoughts and minds as we
grapple with doubt, anxiety, and fear. Thoughts of generosity are
often met with fiery darts of doubt and insecurity. We may hear
from the Lord about what we should give, but quickly our minds

are flooded with rational thoughts, and our own insecurities default us to inaction. We see Moses respond this way when the Lord asked him to go to Egypt to free the Israelites. Instead of responding in faith, Moses asked God to send someone else because he was of poor speech (Exodus 4:10-16). Moses' insecurity tried to prevent the Lord's calling.

Physical battles take place around us when people or situations arise that attempt to distract, agitate, or engulf us. Daniel faced this as the rulers of Babylon plotted to throw him into the lion's den (Daniel 6).

Finally, we experience emotional battles in the form of stress, anxiety, tension, or depression. David likely suffered from extreme stress and anxiety before fleeing to Ziklag to avoid capture by Saul (1 Samuel 27:1). No matter the source—whether internal, physical, or emotional—as Christians, we are instructed not to fear.

> So do not fear, for I am with you; do not be dismayed, for I am your God. I will strengthen you and help you; I will uphold you with my righteous right hand. (Isaiah 41:10)

Jesus' presence is the primary reason we are not to be afraid. On the side of the High King of heaven and with the Commander of heaven's armies, we have confidence that we will be victorious, knowing the greater battle is already won. Though we live from victory, our life is not without struggles. Opposition rises to distract us from purpose, frighten us from obedience, and soften us into inaction. Generosity is a powerful weapon in our arsenal, but as we activate it, we often encounter opposition. Let me illustrate with a few examples.

FINANCIAL OPPOSITION

My friend Kyle is one of my favorite people in the world. We always seem to be on the same page about everything. I think everyone needs a friend like Kyle in their life. As I embarked on my own journey with generosity, he was there to witness it from afar. After hearing multiple testimonies and seeing the supernatural ways God provided and blessed my life, Kyle, a highly successful banker in New York City, decided to take it upon himself to give a year-end offering to God as a thank you for His provision over the previous year. A couple years ago, he told me how he was excited to give to God and step into generosity.

Shortly after taking this step of faith, one of his accounts was hacked, wiping out his entire crypto portfolio. Gone. Less than a month after stepping out in faith with his generosity financially—it was the biggest gift he had ever given God—he was the victim of a financial attack. Undeterred, Kyle pressed on, knowing that he was stepping into something more important than any earthly treasure. He was making an impact for eternity.

Despite the attack, Kyle continued to operate in generosity. It confirmed his faith and inspired him to step into even greater trust in God. As a result, he has made it a yearly habit to give a first fruits offering to the Lord, a practice continually reminding him to walk in obedience and advance the kingdom. Kyle told me he considered it a privilege to be attacked because it showed he was on the offense—the enemy doesn't waste attacks on those sitting on the sidelines. Through this faith-filled obedience, Kyle has seen God pour out favor at work. He is consistently a top performer, his finances continue to increase, and, more importantly, his faith has grown deeper. What the enemy meant for harm, God used to build unshakable faith and usher Kyle into the true abundance found only in Christ. He has fully surrendered his calling in finance to God, and in doing so has been freed from the anxiety that dominates this high-stress field. Today, he rests secure, knowing that God—not money—is his ultimate provider.

Another example is my friend Kris, who is a missionary to the nations. He lives in Hawaii and regularly travels the world evangelizing and leading crusades for Christ. He and his wife have three boys. Before they were pregnant with their third, Kris felt the

Lord leading them to buy a home and that God would provide for their needs.

As a missionary, his family relies fully on God's support daily. If you don't know much about housing prices in Hawaii... well, it's not cheap! After a visit stateside and years of prayer, God was finally positioning Kris and his wife to buy a home. They found one they liked and were ready to open escrow. After wiring the initial money deposit, Kris was contacted by his bank. They received fraudulent wiring instructions and were the victim of a scam. Their entire initial deposit was gone.

Losing this huge chunk of money cost them their house. They could no longer afford to buy. Kris began working side jobs in construction and entered a difficult season of faith stretching with God. However, the financial setback was only temporary, as Kris worked tirelessly to partner with God in belief and action. A year later, they saved enough for another down payment and are now living in a beautiful home in Hawaii with their family of five.

OPPOSITION TO TIME AND TALENTS

When I began writing this book and dedicating my time to completing it, my life entered a whole new season of crazy that I had never experienced. During a span of about two months, my neighbor sued me, my grandpa passed away, and to top it all off, we discovered fleas in our house—and we don't even have pets! It felt like every spare moment I found was suddenly occupied. My life, which once was predictable and peaceful, was suddenly turned upside down. What happened? I purposed in my heart to finish writing this book, but it felt like something kept getting in the way. The time I tried allocating disappeared; it was a struggle up to every deadline. Inspired by Kyle's story of his generosity with his finances, I made efforts to continue on the path and not let the distractions of the lawsuit or fleas get in the way. I was not about to let the opposition to my time prevent me from what I knew the Lord called me to do.

In early 2025, my wife decided to volunteer in the two-year-olds' class at our church. After texting the leader and being scheduled for Sunday, the day before she was to start, our car's transmission blew! Since we only had one car, she didn't have a way to get to church. It was in the shop for nearly two weeks, but once we eventually received our car and she began working in the Sunday school group, the connection was clear—her choice to dedicate her time was met with resistance.

When my friend, Laura, started her Mac & Jesus ministry, it was far from easy. Upon sharing her idea with a few friends, she was welcomed with skepticism, doubt, and raised eyebrows. *Why would you do that? How does that help?* Many questions came from those closest to her from within her church community. On the first night she planned to go out; every single person who said they would join bailed at the last minute. Desperate for help, both spiritually and more so practically (just lifting and moving that much macaroni and cheese is not easy), Laura called her good friend from Santa Barbara, who made the three-hour drive down to Orange County to help.

What caused all these setbacks—from Kyle's generous offering to the opposition to Kris' home purchase to the attack on time when I wrote this book to the opposition to Emma's volunteering to Laura's friends bailing last minute after she stepped out in faith to launch a new ministry? Though Jesus is on the throne, there is an active war at play in our lives and around us. We must be cognizant of and equipped for this war as we step into a life of generosity.

THE ARMOR OF GOD: TOOLS FOR VICTORY

I had heard of spiritual warfare, but I never really understood the power structure of the demonic until studying the Bible more deeply. Paul gives us insight into this power hierarchy in Ephesians.

For our struggle is not against flesh and blood, but against the rulers, against the authorities, against the powers of this dark world and against the spiritual forces of evil in the heavenly realms. (Ephesians 6:12)

Based on this verse, we learn there is a governmental structure within the demonic kingdom that aligns with Satan. In the book of Daniel, we see more evidence of this demonic kingdom. When Daniel receives a revelation, or vision, he is so disturbed that he begins a three-week fast. At the culmination of the fast, he is visited by an angel, sent to explain what will happen, and gives us important insight into the heavenly realm.

Then he continued, "Do not be afraid, Daniel. Since the first day that you set your mind to gain understanding and to humble yourself before your God, your words were heard, and I have come in response to them. But the prince of the Persian kingdom resisted me twenty-one days. Then Michael, one of the chief princes, came to help me, because I was detained there with the king of Persia." (Daniel 10:12-13)

The angel responded the moment Daniel humbled himself three weeks prior but was caught up by the prince of the Persian kingdom, which we know is a demonic force because it opposed the angel who was sent in response to God. There is constant warfare in the heavenly places, and this passage illustrates that the angel was caught up in a fight, a struggle. This demonic prince held authority in a region that was part of the demonic kingdom and aligned with the Persian kingdom.

Based on this passage and Paul's letter in Ephesians, we catch a glimpse of the demonic. We know there are rulers, authorities, and powers and that these demons even have strongholds they claim as their rule, which are tied to physical land on earth. I find it fascinating how the angel was sent the moment Daniel humbled himself. I wonder how often we feel like God is delaying an answer to prayer when, in reality, the answer was already sent, and a battle is being fought to deliver it.

The idea of spiritual strongholds or assignments over towns, cities, or regions was new to me, but it made so much sense. When I moved to Seattle in 2016, my mom, dad, and brother came out to visit me in the fall. They wanted to see the leaves change colors—something that doesn't happen with palm trees in sunny California. I planned for us to go on a hike, explore downtown, see the famous Pike Place Fish Market, and take an underground tour. I heard Seattle had a unique underground tour tied to its city history. In 1889, the Great Seattle Fire destroyed the entire downtown district in a day. Instead of fully rebuilding what was destroyed, they raised the level of the city. To this day, if you go downtown, you can still see some of the early city settlement by going underground at a few locations. We took the tour, but we were shocked at what we learned.

On the tour, we discovered more details about the fire. It had something to do with glue catching fire next to a wood shop, which set off a crazy sequence of events that ultimately led to the city's destruction. However, upon rebuilding, the city was in desperate need of money. At the time, there was an infamous woman running a brothel in Seattle. It was a well-known and heavily trafficked establishment, considering Seattle was a small fishing town. To raise money for the city's rebuilding, the city leaders essentially chose to ignore the Madame's operation and tax it instead—even though prostitution was illegal. The city quickly raised funds and was rebuilt by heavily leveraging this new income source. Unfortunately, this decision—likely made in ignorance of spiritual realities—made a lasting impact I believe is still evident today.

You can even see it in the DNA of Seattle. Sexual confusion and perversion are rampant. I believe that when the city partnered with the madame running the brothel, the city, perhaps unknowingly, gave authority to the demonic to establish a presence and stronghold. While living in Seattle, I found myself struggling with issues that I had never encountered. That first year, I was depressed but had no idea why; I had never felt it before. I understood that we are more than overcomers and have authority in Christ, but the spiritual atmosphere of the region weighed on me.

Similarly, when I moved to NYC, I suddenly felt incredibly stressed about money. Several times, I happily gave away all I had in my bank account in response to God's word, but somehow in NYC, I found myself thinking about money regularly. I thought about how I could make more, how nice it would be to have more, and what I would do if I had more. The thought of money was present in a way unlike ever before. I believe a spirit of greed, among others, has a hold on that city, given its historical ties to the stock market and financial institutions. Now, this isn't to say that these regions are still held by the demonic today. I honestly do not know how it works. All I can tell you is that in those two places, I felt weighed down by depression and stressed about money more than anywhere else I've lived.

Spiritual warfare isn't theoretical or regional—it can become deeply personal. In our own lives, Emma and I experienced this firsthand on several occasions. Two years after we got married, we had a baby boy, Wess. Emma labored for nearly forty hours and, after pushing for four hours with no breakthrough, ultimately underwent an emergency C-section.

In the operating room, Wess was born, but something was wrong. His breathing was irregular, and he wasn't crying like he should have been. He was immediately rushed to the NICU and placed on a breathing tube. Emma had an infection, so the doctors weren't sure if Wess was fighting the same infection or if something else was happening. Emma lost a lot of blood, and the doctors weren't sure if she needed a transfusion.

It was a stressful couple of days in the hospital trying to care for the two people I loved most—each recovering from significant medical events in separate rooms. I got very little sleep, and we rallied prayer from friends and family. Slowly, the good news started to come in. Emma wouldn't need a transfusion and was recovering well. But the best news of all: Wess didn't have an infection and was growing stronger. After two days, the doctors removed the breathing tube, and Wess was discharged from the NICU.

One of the most eye-opening truths Emma has shared with me is that the devil often attacks our calling. From the start, Emma and I both felt God has plans for Wess to be a worship leader. At his baby dedication, the pastor praying over him prophesied that he would become a worship leader—even though we never shared the word we both received. That moment further confirmed what we believed for Wess, deepening our excitement and anticipation to see him walk in the fullness of his calling.

My best friend Kyle is another example. He excelled as a collegiate quarterback, setting records on the field. His success in sports was the very thing that led him to realize his true calling: finance. At his wedding a couple of years ago, his dad, Randy, shared a powerful story about Kyle's birth. When Kyle was born, his right hand and arm were pinned against his side in an unnatural way. As soon as he came out of the womb, Randy was shocked—Kyle's arm was blue and purple. It was ultimately this right arm of his that was recruited, given a football scholarship, promoted to starter, and set records, all leading to landing his dream job, where he makes a great influence for the kingdom of heaven.

Kyle's story is a reminder that the devil often attacks us in the very areas where God plans to use us most. The same is true for Wess, whose early struggles made us even more certain of the purpose God has for his life. To this day, Wess loves music. And just like God used Kyle's arm—originally thought to be a weakness—to propel him into influence and achievement as a quarterback and eventually into his true calling of finance, Emma and I are excited to see what God does through Wess' worship and the power of his lungs.

All of this confirmed something Emma and I believe deeply. When we walk in obedience to our calling, fueled by generosity and bold faith, we will inevitably face opposition. The enemy doesn't stay idle. He strikes at the heart of our purpose. We must understand that we are in a battle if we are to win. Too many Christians fail to fight because they don't fully understand who they're fighting or how to engage. Let me be clear: our adversary is cunning, deliberate, and evil beyond our imagination. He seeks to destroy us, and he doesn't play fair: "Be alert and of sober mind. Your enemy the devil prowls around like a roaring lion looking for someone to devour" (1 Peter 5:8).

Though the devil wants to see us destroyed, the good news is we already have the tools to win! Paul shows us how we as Christians are supposed to fight in 2 Corinthians 10 and Ephesians 6.

For though we live in the world, we do not wage war as the world does. The weapons we fight with are not the weapons of the world. On the contrary, they have divine power to demolish strongholds. We demolish arguments and every pretension that sets itself up against the knowledge of God, and we take captive every thought to make it obedient to Christ. And we will be ready to punish every act of disobedience, once your obedience is complete. (2 Corinthians 10:3-6)

Finally, be strong in the Lord and in his mighty power. Put on the full armor of God, so that you can take your stand against the devil's schemes. For our struggle is not against flesh and blood, but against the rulers, against the authorities, against the powers of this dark world and against the spiritual forces of evil in the heavenly realms. Therefore put on the full armor of God, so that when the day of evil comes, you may be able to stand your ground, and after you have done everything, to stand. Stand firm then, with the belt of truth buckled around your waist, with the breastplate of righteousness in place, and with your feet fitted with the readiness that comes from the gospel of peace. In addition to all this, take up the shield of faith, with which you can extinguish all the flaming arrows of the evil one. Take the helmet of salvation and the sword of the Spirit, which is the word of God. And pray in the Spirit on all occasions with all kinds of prayers and requests. With this in mind, be alert and always keep on praying for all the Lord's people. (Ephesians 6:10-18)

EMBRACING THE SPIRITUAL BATTLE

I am still learning how to fight back. It's important as we fight to realize that our battle is not of flesh and blood but in the spiritual realm. What this means is our battle is not against the people who stand in our way but the demonic forces empowering them. Jesus shows this can even come from people close to us: "Jesus turned and said to Peter, 'Get behind me, Satan! You are a stumbling block to me; you do not have in mind the concerns of God, but merely human concerns'" (Matthew 16:23).

We must take up spiritual tools to fight if we are to win. We must fight with Scripture, prayer, fasting, verse memorization, words of encouragement, attending church, tithing, and giving. Our weapons look vastly different from how the world fights. We must trust Jesus, the great Commander of heaven's armies, to wage war on our behalf as we call on His name.

Now when Joshua was near Jericho, he looked up and saw a man standing in front of him with a drawn sword in his hand. Joshua went up to him and asked, "Are you for us or for our enemies?" "Neither," he replied, "but as commander of the army of the LORD I have now come." Then Joshua fell facedown to the ground in reverence, and asked him, "What message does my Lord have for his servant?" The commander of the LORD's army replied, "Take off your sandals, for the place where you are standing is holy." And Joshua did so. (Joshua 5:13-15)

I saw heaven standing open and there before me was a white horse, whose rider is called Faithful and True. With justice he judges and wages war. His eyes are like blazing fire, and on his head are many crowns. He has a name written on him that no one knows but he himself. He is dressed in a robe dipped in blood, and his name is the Word of God. The armies of heaven were following him, riding on white horses and dressed in fine linen, white and clean. Coming out of his mouth is a sharp sword with which to strike down the nations. "He will rule them with an iron scepter." He treads the winepress of the fury of the wrath of God Almighty. On his robe and on his thigh he has this name written: KING OF KINGS AND LORD OF LORDS. (Revelation 19:11-16)

As we learn to fight in the spirit, we make an impact in the physical realm. One thing I have learned over the years is the devil does not have self-control. As Satan attempts to tempt, thwart, obstruct, confuse, steal, kill, or destroy the plans for good over our lives, when we resist, he flees! Self-control and patience are fruits of the Spirit. As such, we know that the devil does not have either. He does not waste his time when he is losing and instead moves on to a new target.

One of my favorite stories that inspires me to lead a godly life fully surrendered to Jesus is in Acts 19. Here we see that Paul is not only well-known on earth (and likely in heaven) but also amongst the demons! His impact was so great the demons knew his name due to the damage he was inflicting on their kingdom.

God did extraordinary miracles through Paul, so that even hand-kerchiefs and aprons that had touched him were taken to the sick, and their illnesses were cured and the evil spirits left them. Some Jews who went around driving out evil spirits tried to invoke the name of the Lord Jesus over those who were demon-possessed. They would say, "In the name of the Jesus whom Paul preaches, I command you to come out." Seven sons of Sceva, a Jewish chief priest, were doing this. One day the evil spirit answered them, "Jesus I know, and Paul I know about, but who are you?" Then the man who had the evil spirit jumped on them and overpowered them all. He gave them such a beating that they ran out of the house naked and bleeding. When this became known to the Jews and Greeks living in Ephesus, they were all seized with fear, and the name of the Lord Jesus was held in high honor. Many of those who believed now came and openly confessed what they had done. A number who had practiced sorcery brought their scrolls together and burned them publicly. When they calculated the value of the scrolls, the total came to fifty thousand drachmas. In this way the word of the Lord spread widely and grew in power. (Acts 19:11-20)

Paul was so obedient in word and deed to the commission of Jesus that the spiritual realm, specifically the demonic, took notice. At times, I like to imagine I am walking so in step with the Spirit and advancing ground that the devil and his demons are frustrated as their losses mount. When we see salvations, healings, evangelism, love, generosity, and words of encouragement pour out of the lives of believers, the devil and his demons lose ground! We cannot choose whether we want to enter the battle—it comes to us—but we can choose what type of soldier we will be. Let us be good soldiers, who fight with courage, follow Jesus closely, and lead effectively.

During a particularly heavy war-fighting season, Jesus gave me this revelation. The closer we are to the front lines, the safer we are! We see this truth, as Jesus Himself was ahead of the armies of Israel, leading them into battle. This theme is evident in the Exodus as well, as God travelled before the Israelites by pillar of cloud by day and pillar of fire by night.

By day the LORD went ahead of them in a pillar of cloud to guide them on their way and by night in a pillar of fire to give them light, so that they could travel by day or night. Neither the pillar of cloud by day nor the pillar of fire by night left its place in front of the people. (Exodus 13:21-22)

As our High King, Jesus plays the role of protector. It's our King's job to protect His people in battle.

> The LORD your God, who is going before you, will fight for you, as he did for you in Egypt, before your very eyes. (Deuteronomy 1:30)

> But you will not leave in haste or go in flight; for the LORD will go before you, the God of Israel will be your rear guard. (Isaiah 52:12)

This theme is recurring throughout the Old Testament as the Lord regularly fights for His people. The most striking example of the Lord going before the army of Israel into battle is found in 2 Samuel 5 as David prepares to attack the Philistine army. The Lord gives him instructions and a specific war strategy, but David is to wait for the Lord to go into battle first. In war times, the safest place to be is at the front lines because there we are closest to Jesus!

PARTNERING WITH JESUS IN VICTORY

What a privilege it is to partner with Jesus in literally advancing His kingdom into new territory through our generosity. I am reminded of Paul's charge to Timothy: "Timothy, my son, I am giving you this command in keeping with the prophecies once made about you, so that by recalling them you may fight the battle well" (1 Timothy 1:18).

As we are faithful in our finances, obedient in our actions, fully surrendered in heart, trustworthy in deed, responsible in stewardship, and overflowing with love, we become vessels capable of reflecting the glory God deserves through our lives and become trusted partners with Him.

Despite the threat of the enemy, we know we are overcomers.

One of my favorite passages is found in Isaiah 14, where the prophet describes Lucifer.

> How you are fallen from heaven, O Lucifer, son of the morning! *How* you are cut down to the ground, you who weakened the nations! For you have said in your heart: "I will ascend into heaven, I will exalt my throne above the stars of God; I will also sit on the mount of the congregation on the farthest sides of the north; I will ascend above the heights of the clouds, I will be like the Most High." Yet you shall be brought down to Sheol, to the lowest depths of the Pit. (Isaiah 14:12-15 NKJV)

What I love about this passage—jumping down to verses 16 and 17—is how it frames our final perspective of the enemy.

> Those who see you will gaze at you *and* consider you, *saying*: "Is this the man who made the earth tremble, who shook kingdoms, who made the world as a wilderness and destroyed its cities, *who* did not open the house of his prisoners?"

It's almost as if, once we are fully present with Jesus in heaven, we will look down on Lucifer—the devil—and think, "Is this really the guy? Is that him? That's it? All this from him? He's a nobody!" I imagine we will be so shocked at how frail, weak, and powerless he truly is. We often imagine a big, bad devil on par with our Savior, Jesus, but the reality is the battle was already won. The devil is defeated. Jesus is victorious. We are crowned with Him in glory and seated with Him at the right hand of the Father.

As we enter war seasons, our knowledge of the enemy becomes more intimate. We begin to understand his tactics and anticipate his moves. The cloud of uncertainty and fear surrounding an unknown enemy fades, and the face of our adversary becomes clear. From this place of clarity, we are empowered to partner with Jesus in His warfare—after we have stood our ground.

In this fight, we move beyond simply withstanding the devil; we advance with the Lord of heaven's armies—and we do this through our generosity. We bring the battle to the enemy and take ground for the kingdom. We become soldiers with Christ—battle-tested, trustworthy, faithful, generous, self-controlled, and disciplined. And in living the life of a soldier, we live fully open. Readily deployable and with open hands, we live the simple life of a soldier who is required to do nothing else but simply obey the commanding officer. It is no longer we who live but Christ who lives in us. The freedom we unlock allows us to bring the battle wherever we are called to go, knowing that we have already won, as our intimacy with the Father guides us each step of the way.

Though opposition may come as we step into our kingdom calling and a lifestyle of kingdom generosity, we know that we do so from a place of victory. Battles will be waged, but victory is guaranteed. The mental, physical, and spiritual attacks coming our way are best fought in partnership with Jesus and the Holy Spirit, who indwells us. We must not shy away from the battle but fully embrace it as we know the abundant life—ever-serving, ever-advancing, ever-pleasing to our Lord and Savior—is within reach as we fight for His kingdom to come.

7

GIVING AS WORSHIP

Worship the LORD with gladness.

PSALM 100:2

What is worship? Have you ever asked yourself this simple question? I find myself wrestling with it frequently. Worship is more than singing praise songs. It's more than offering sacrifices (giving tithes and offerings). It's more than walking in obedience. So, what is it? Romans 12:1 gives us a glimpse:

> Therefore, I urge you, brothers and sisters, in view of God's mercy, to offer your bodies as a living sacrifice, holy and pleasing to God—this is your true and proper worship.

I've heard it expressed that anything can be worship if done with the right heart posture. We can worship through the way we attend church, work, live, eat, serve others, and give.

Our lives are living worship. When we work, we can worship. When we fellowship, we can worship. When we rest, we can worship. When we eat and drink, we can worship (1 Corinthians

10:31). As we offer ourselves as living sacrifices and pursue a life-style of kingdom generosity, our entire lives can become an act of worship. We bring worship with us as a flower carries a sweet scent once blossomed. Living lives in full bloom attached to the vine of Christ, we bring His pleasing aroma everywhere.

> For we are to God the pleasing aroma of Christ among those who are being saved and those who are perishing. To the one we are an aroma that brings death; to the other, an aroma that brings life. And who is equal to such a task? (2 Corinthians 2:15-16).

A couple years ago, my wife and I went to visit The Flower Fields in Carlsbad, California. Right off the freeway, for much of the year, the fields are barren and useless. However, if you visit from March through May, you see an explosion of color, rows upon rows of blossoming flowers, and fragrant aromas filling the air.

Unlike these flowers, our life of kingdom generosity doesn't fade once summer begins. Deeply rooted, our generosity produces a pleasing aroma wherever we go and fresh life to all those we reach as we live out of a place of worship. Immune to life's circumstances, our worship is continual, never ceasing as we water ourselves in the Word of God daily.

Operating out of abundance, the field in Carlsbad has more than enough flowers to give away and still allow others to experience the beauty. As they sell flowers, the impact on the field is unnoticed as the sheer size of the bloom overwhelms visitors. So too, as we blossom in our generosity, our giving doesn't leave us empty but rather shares what's beautiful (Jesus) with the world around us.

But don't just take my word for it! The Bible provides several examples of giving from a place of such overflow as an act of worship.

CAIN AND ABEL

Cain was the first offspring of Adam and Eve, the eldest son. At this time, though banished from the Garden of Eden and the right to the tree of life, the Lord still fellowshipped with the family of Adam, Eve, Cain, and Abel.

> So the LORD God banished him from the Garden of Eden to work the ground from which he had been taken. After he drove the man out, he placed on the east side of the Garden of Eden cherubim and a flaming sword flashing back and forth to guard the way to the tree of life. (Genesis 3:23-24)

It's safe to assume that, since the way back to the tree of life was physically blocked by the cherubim and flaming sword, the family still brought offerings to the Lord in person. We see this in the story of Cain and Abel, who both presented offerings to the Lord. Whether this was part of a regular occurrence—weekly, monthly, yearly, or some other interval—we do not know. What we do know is that they presented offerings to the Lord.

> Now Abel kept flocks, and Cain worked the soil. In the course of time Cain brought some of the fruits of the soil as an offering to the LORD. And Abel also brought an offering—fat portions from some of the firstborn of his flock. The LORD looked with favor on Abel and his offering, but on Cain and his offering he did not look with favor. So Cain was very angry, and his face was downcast. Then the LORD said to Cain, "Why are you angry? Why is your face downcast? If you do what is right, will you not be accepted? But if you do not do what is right, sin is crouching at your door; it desires to have you, but you must rule over it." Now Cain said to his brother Abel, "Let's go out to the field." While they were in the field, Cain attacked his brother Abel and killed him. Then

the LORD said to Cain, "Where is your brother Abel?" "I don't know," he replied. "Am I my brother's keeper?" The LORD said, "What have you done? Listen! Your brother's blood cries out to me from the ground." (Genesis 4:2-10)

Cain worked the soil, and Abel worked with livestock. Both brought offerings, but one was not accepted: Cain's. Have you wondered why Cain's offering was not accepted? I have. Perhaps he offered fruits that were rotten, old, or lesser in quality or quantity. We know that God is just, so it certainly could not have been that He preferred meat over vegetables. All the Bible tells us is that the Lord preferred Abel's sacrifice over Cain's.

It's wise to surmise that Abel brought forth the best from his flocks—unblemished, perfect, spotless—while Cain did not. Abel gave his best, while Cain likely brought his worst. Abel eagerly brought to the Lord the best of what his hands produced, as a child excitedly showing their father a school project, while Cain last-minute grabbed some scraps for the offering. The offering likely cost Abel much monetarily, and Cain, potentially less. The hearts behind the sacrifice were vastly different, although the actions were similar.

Unfortunately, Abel's generous offering, which so pleased God, was one of the last acts of his life. From there, out of the seed of comparison, bitterness sprang up and blossomed in Cain. He took vengeance on his brother out of jealousy over the Lord's favor that Abel found. The offering Abel provided so touched the heart of God that Jesus includes him among the martyrs. Abel died for his faith. Jesus confirms this in Luke:

Therefore this generation will be held responsible for the blood of all the prophets that has been shed since the beginning of the world, from the blood of Abel to the blood of Zechariah, who was killed between the altar and the sanctuary. Yes, I tell you, this generation will be held responsible for it all. (Luke 11:50-51)

The great hall of faith chapter captures this generous offering that led to Abel's demise: "By faith Abel brought God a better offering than Cain did. By faith he was commended as righteous, when God spoke well of his offerings. And by faith Abel still speaks, even though he is dead" (Hebrews 11:4).

Abel's actions still speak. We know they do, as his actions thousands of years ago in generosity still spark our hearts to that same faith the prophet discovered.

THE WISE MEN

Perhaps no men in history have traveled farther or in harsher conditions than the wise men who journeyed to bring young Jesus gifts of gold, frankincense, and myrrh. The wise men traveled from the East. Whether that was Persia, India, or China, we do not know. What we do know is they closely studied the times, awaiting a Savior. By studying the cosmos, these wise men were led to a man, the Savior—the most precious discovery one can make. These men studied and acted. They put their faith into action by going to find the King of the Jews and worshiping Him.

> After Jesus was born in Bethlehem in Judea, during the time of King Herod, Magi from the east came to Jerusalem and asked, "Where is the one who has been born king of the Jews? We saw his star when it rose and have come to worship him." (Matthew 2:1-2)

They came from afar to worship Him, but what did their worship entail? Gifts of gold, frankincense, and myrrh. Gold represented His royal authority and kingship, frankincense represented His divinity and priestly role, and myrrh symbolized His humanity—especially His death and burial to come. Oh, what a prophetic gift of worship! Through this gifting, we also see a foreshadowing of the Trinity. What understanding did these wise men have even then, before the complete Bible or the full picture of salvation? How did they, though so far physically, manage to draw so close to the Savior of the universe spiritually? Many in Christ's own town, even His own family, rejected Him, yet these wise men acknowledged Him as King before He even spoke a word. What testimony did they return to their native land with about the goodness and kindness of the Messiah, though He was only a small child?

Yet, to receive anything *from* Him, the wise men brought their best *to* Him. Knowing the goodness of God, I imagine these men were richly blessed for the remainder of their lives. May we have wise men who again traverse lands far and wide, cross barren places, study in expectation, and travel with their brothers and sisters to bring such gifts to our Savior.

THE QUEEN OF SHEBA

One of my favorite passages is when the Queen of Sheba comes to visit the famed king of Israel, King Solomon. As word spread throughout the ancient world of a wise and rich king—so wealthy that there was no silver found at his table, only gold—one queen was so intrigued by the legends she decided to visit for herself to see if it was true. Leaving from modern Yemen or Ethiopia, the Queen of Sheba embarked on a journey from her kingdom to Israel to learn from King Solomon. How wise is the person who, like the Queen of Sheba, is willing to leave his or her kingdom of comfort, achievement, and success to pursue the King of Kings and hear His truths?

What a powerful picture this is—not just of heartfelt worship, but of prophecy fulfilled. The Queen's act of bringing treasures to Solomon gives us a physical image of spiritual devotion. But even more, it demonstrates the divine answer to a king's prayer recorded in Psalm 72—a prayer likely spoken during Solomon's early reign:

May the kings of Tarshish and of distant shores bring tribute to him. May the kings of Sheba and Seba present him gifts... Long may he live! May gold from Sheba be given him. May people ever pray for him and bless him all day long. (Psalm 72:10, 15)

Likely at his coronation, Psalm 72 details a humble prayer early in Solomon's kingship petitioning the Lord for justice and prosperity for Israel. It is in 1 Kings 10 and 2 Chronicles 9 where we find the fulfillment of that prayer.

When the queen of Sheba heard about the fame of Solomon and his relationship to the Lord, she came to test Solomon with hard questions. Arriving at Jerusalem with a very great caravan—with camels carrying spices, large quantities of gold, and precious stones—she came to Solomon and talked with him about all that she had on her mind. Solomon answered all her questions; nothing was too hard for the king to explain to her... She said to the king, "The report I heard in my own country about your achievements and your wisdom is true. But I did not believe these things until I came and saw with my own eyes. Indeed, not even half was told me; in wisdom and wealth you have far exceeded the report I heard. How happy your people must be! How happy your officials, who continually stand before you and hear your wisdom! Praise be to the LORD your God, who has delighted in you and placed you on the throne of Israel. Because of the LORD's eternal love for Israel, he has made you king to maintain justice and righteousness." (1 Kings 10:1-3, 6-9)

Upon coming to Solomon with the intention to test him and speak her mind, she finds Solomon's wisdom is sufficient to answer it all—nothing was too hard for him. How blessed we are when we bring our hard questions, the truths we are wrestling with, and everything on our mind to our King Jesus. I love how the Old Testament provides a physical picture of a spiritual truth.

Much can be learned from this exchange if we put ourselves in the place of the Queen of Sheba, with Jesus playing the role of Solomon. After finding peace for every thought on her mind, she observes the scene, or goodness of God, and is so awed, so floored, so inspired—she's overwhelmed.

> When the queen of Sheba saw all the wisdom of Solomon and the palace he had built, the food on his table, the seating of his officials, the attending servants in their robes, his cupbearers, and the burnt offerings he made at the temple of the LORD, she was overwhelmed. (1 Kings 10:4-5).

How many of us had the same response when we fully surrendered to the Lord and realized His abundant goodness? The Queen of Sheba is so moved by the vast extravagance of Israel's king of Israel that she blesses him with a royal bounty.

> And she gave the king 120 talents of gold, large quantities of spices, and precious stones. Never again were so many spices brought in as those the queen of Sheba gave to King Solomon. (1 Kings 10:10)

The version in 2 Chronicles 9:12 highlights my favorite part of the story.

> King Solomon gave the queen of Sheba all she desired and asked for; he gave her more than she had brought to him. Then she left and returned with her retinue to her own country.

Oh, how I love that part! The Queen of Sheba (a picture of you and me) visits Solomon (a picture of Jesus) with a royal bounty from her treasures, but she leaves with even more than she brought. Perhaps the most beautiful part is this: before the Queen of Sheba ever responded, a king was already praying for her.

When we bring the best of our treasures to our King, Jesus,

watch as what we intended to be a blessing to the Lord turns into a blessing for ourselves. The Queen of Sheba left the most blessed, receiving back more than she gave. So too, as you and I bring the best of our treasures to Jesus, it is we who are the most blessed— returning to our own lands to tell of His goodness: the gospel.

8

_____

HOLY GENEROSITY

*How abundant are the good things that you have
stored up for those who fear you, that you bestow
in the sight of all, on those who take refuge
in you.*

PSALM 31:19

Kingdom generosity not only changes our hearts; it also moves the heart of God. God loves His children so much that He died to set us free, but He doesn't want us to stop at salvation. He wants to transform us into His likeness and character. As we grow and catch His vision for generosity, it captures His attention. One of the ways we do this is through our giving.

Following Jesus' example, we see that He is wildly generous. Possessing the fullness of heaven, He humbled himself to the point of death so that we can become co-heirs with Him, sharing in His glory: "Now if we are children, then we are heirs—heirs of God and co-heirs with Christ, if indeed we share in his sufferings in order that we may also share in his glory" (Romans 8:17).

What a privilege it is to be called a brother or sister of Christ and a co-heir in His kingdom—an expression of generosity we may never fully fathom this side of eternity. God generously brings us into His kingdom reign and gives us possession over His kingdom! Just as a co-heir receives part of a trust, Christ Himself freely invites us to reign with Him. From creation, God's divine plan to reign with us was on display in the Garden of Eden: "God blessed them and said to them, 'Be fruitful and increase in number; fill the earth and subdue it. Rule over the fish in the sea and the birds in the sky and over every living creature that moves on the ground'" (Genesis 1:29).

Starting in the first chapter of Genesis, we see the heart of generosity God has for His children. He created all things, owns all things, and sustains all things (Acts 17:28). Yet He wants to share all things with His children. It gives God great delight to freely give to His kids, as generosity is core to His character. But when God's children respond generously and catch the vision of kingdom generosity, there is a collision of the supernatural and the natural that so moves the heart of God He can't help but respond.

EXPRESSIONS OF HOLY GENEROSITY

There is a form of generosity we rarely see today in Western societies—holy generosity. It's a generosity so pure, so extravagant, born from such a loving heart, that it actually moves the heart of God. This is extravagant giving, where the Lord is so undone by an expression of faith that He is moved to respond. We see several examples of this type of generosity throughout Scripture.

The Woman with the Alabaster Jar

In perhaps the most famous example, we have the woman who poured out the alabaster jar of perfume on Jesus' feet. This scene appears in three of the four Gospels. Here is Matthew's version:

While he was in Bethany, reclining at the table in the home of Simon the Leper, a woman came with an alabaster jar of very expensive perfume, made of pure nard. She broke the jar and poured the perfume on his head. Some of those present were saying indignantly to one another, "Why this waste of perfume? It could have been sold for more than a year's wages and the money given to the poor." And they rebuked her harshly. "Leave her alone," said Jesus. "Why are you bothering her? She has done a beautiful thing to me. The poor you will always have with you, and you can help them any time you want. But you will not always have me. She did what she could. She poured perfume on my body beforehand to prepare for my burial. Truly I tell you, wherever the gospel is preached throughout the world, what she has done will also be told, in memory of her." (Mark 14:3-9)

Did you catch that? This act of holy generosity was so extravagant and so moved the heart of Jesus that He not only called it beautiful but also declared that wherever His gospel is preached throughout the world, this story would be told. I like to picture Him telling His disciples, "Write this down. This is an expression of love and generosity that must be remembered."

In the United States, the median household income is approximately $75,000 (based on 2025 data). Imagine a complete year's wages poured out as a gift at the feet of our Savior to prepare Him for burial. The TV show The Chosen wonderfully captures this scene. We do not know the woman's financial situation, but we can infer without a doubt that the gift was beyond extravagant, as Jesus' response indicates.

David and the Temple

David is commonly known as a man after God's own heart. We get this notion from 1 Samuel 13:14, where Samuel tells Saul, "But now your kingdom will not endure; the LORD has sought out a man after his own heart and appointed him ruler of his people, because you have not kept the LORD's command."

When we think of David, we often think of the story of David and Goliath or David and Bathsheba. I've heard people say, "Well, David sinned too, and he was a man after God's own heart." However, we forget the extent of David's radical devotion to the Lord.

David fought lions and bears in the wilderness to protect his sheep from being preyed upon. He took in the outcasts and strangers, training them in the way they should go, while instilling purpose and community during his days in the wilderness. He humbly served in the courts of kings as a musician, offering his full energy toward serving the king whom he was anointed to replace. He fought wars for King Saul to expand and protect his kingdom and was even assigned captain of the armed men (1 Samuel 18:5). He refused to lay a hand upon Saul when he had the chance to strike him down in a cave. He wrote many of the psalms, pouring out his heart to the Lord. He was a conqueror, warrior, poet, leader, politician, outcast, shepherd, and friend, as well as a man of deep generosity. Much can be written about the life of David, but one of the most striking character traits of David, in my estimation, was his generosity. We see evidence of his generous heart as he prepares to build the Lord's temple:

> After the king was settled in his palace and the LORD had given him rest from all his enemies around him, he said to Nathan the prophet, "Here I am, living in a house of cedar, while the ark of God remains in a tent." Nathan replied to the king, "Whatever you have in mind, go ahead and do it, for the LORD is with you." (2 Samuel 7:1-3)

David had a deep desire to see the house of God built and established in Israel. He had a passion for the temple and eagerly desired to begin construction, until a word from the Lord informed him that his son, Solomon, was to build it—not David. Despite this word from God, David knew that although he was not to build the temple of the Lord, he could still prepare. Wise is the man or woman who is willing to set aside their dreams and desires and listen to the voice of the Lord, preparing the way for another. David prepared for the temple's construction by giving generously from his own finances to fund the development. We see this story in 1 Chronicles 29:1-5, where, after the word of the Lord came through the prophet Nathan, David gave.

> Then King David said to the whole assembly: "My son Solomon, the one whom God has chosen, is young and inexperienced. The task is great, because this palatial structure is not for man but for the Lord God. With all my resources I have provided for the temple of my God—gold for the gold work, silver for the silver, bronze for the bronze, iron for the iron and wood for the wood, as well as onyx for the settings, turquoise, stones of various colors, and all kinds of fine stone and marble—all of these in large quantities. Besides, in my devotion to the temple of my God I now give my personal treasures of gold and silver for the temple of my God, over and above everything I have provided for this holy temple: three thousand talents of gold (gold of Ophir) and seven thousand talents of refined silver, for the overlaying of the walls of the buildings, for the gold work and the silver work, and for all the work to be done by the craftsmen. Now, who is willing to consecrate themselves to the LORD today?"

Unless you're familiar with the price of gold and silver, this may not mean much to you. After I did the math, based on current market values of gold and silver, this passage took on a whole different meaning.

Material	Weight per Talent	Total Weight (ounces)	2025 Price (per ounce)	Total Value
Gold	75 pounds = 1,200 ounces	3,000 talents x 1,200oz = 3,600,000oz	$3,000	$10.8 billion
Silver	75 pounds = 1,200 ounces	7,000 talents x 1,200oz = 8,400,000oz	$30	$252 million

A talent in biblical times is often estimated to weigh around 75 pounds (or approximately 34 kg).

David personally gave over $11.05 billion (with a "B") to finance the house of the Lord! Now that is extravagant giving. I believe David's extravagant heart of generosity is one of the chief reasons we see him referred to as a man after God's own heart. Far from a reserved or calculated head of state weighing a costly commitment, David was wildly generous toward his King, investing himself without hesitation.

Solomon's Temple Sacrifice

Like David, Solomon had his flaws, but he also had a massive heart of generosity. So much so that the Lord appeared to Solomon two times in response to his giving!

In 1 Kings 3, the Lord appears to Solomon in a dream after he offers a thousand burnt offerings as a sacrifice to the Lord at Gibeon. After orchestrating such a sacrifice, later that night, the Lord appears to Solomon in a dream, telling him to ask for anything and it will be granted. In this famous exchange, Solomon asks the Lord for wisdom to rule the people justly, and God replies that because he did not ask for long life or riches for himself, the Lord was pleased with him, granting his desire along with wealth and honor. Solomon goes on to become likely the richest king in human history, so much so that during his reign silver had little value throughout the kingdom (1 Kings 10:21).

God responded to Solomon's generosity with such an outpouring of blessings that the key asset of his day became worthless! Imagine if God poured out blessings in response to our generosity to the measure that it literally shifted trade markets.

Fast-forward a few years in Solomon's life, and we come to the most impressive example of holy generosity on a massive scale: the dedication of the temple.

When Solomon finished praying, fire came down from heaven and consumed the burnt offering and the sacrifices, and the glory of the LORD filled the temple. The priests could not enter the temple of the LORD because the glory of the LORD filled it. When all the Israelites saw the fire coming down and the glory of the LORD above the temple, they knelt on the pavement with their faces to the ground, and they worshiped and gave thanks to the LORD, saying, "He is good; his love endures forever." Then the king and all the people offered sacrifices before the LORD. And King Solomon offered a sacrifice of twenty-two thousand head of cattle and a hundred and twenty thousand sheep and goats. So the king and all the people dedicated the temple of God. The priests took their positions, as did the Levites with the LORD's musical instruments, which King David had made for praising the LORD and which were used when he gave thanks, saying, "His love endures forever." Opposite the Levites, the priests blew their trumpets, and all the Israelites were standing. Solomon consecrated the middle part of the courtyard in front of the temple of the LORD, and there he offered burnt offerings and the fat of the fellowship offerings, because the bronze altar he had made could not hold the burnt offerings, the grain offerings and the fat portions. (2 Chronicles 7:1-7)

Let's take a closer look at this sacrifice and explore its modern equivalent to better understand this act of holy generosity.

Animal	Average 2025 Price (per head)	Quantity	Total Value (2025)
Cattle	$1,500	22,000	$33 million
Sheep/Goats	$200	120,000	$24 million

91

This adds up to $57 million dedicated upon completion of the temple! What strikes me is this offering came after they had completed the temple (not a cheap project). How often do we provide a sacrifice to the Lord after completing a huge endeavor? Not very. However, Solomon didn't stop at the finished work of the temple; he offered a radical sacrifice to dedicate it to the Lord. We know the Lord was so moved by this display of holy, radical generosity that He visited Solomon once again in a dream, promising Solomon a restorative work that we still pray for to this day.

> When Solomon had finished the temple of the LORD and the royal palace, and had succeeded in carrying out all he had in mind to do in the temple of the LORD and in his own palace, the LORD appeared to him at night and said: "I have heard your prayer and have chosen this place for myself as a temple for sacrifices. When I shut up the heavens so that there is no rain, or command locusts to devour the land or send a plague among my people, if my people, who are called by my name, will humble themselves and pray and seek my face and turn from their wicked ways, then I will hear from heaven, and I will forgive their sin and will heal their land." (2 Chronicles 7:11-14)

God responded to Solomon's first act of generosity with wisdom, wealth, and riches. To Solomon's second act of wild generosity, God provides an eternal promise: "I will hear from heaven, and I will forgive their sin and will heal their land." God's heart was so moved by this act of generosity that countless millions have been blessed, encouraged, and recipients of this promise. How many generations have reaped from the bounty of the land due to the expressive generosity Solomon poured out at the feet of Jesus? The full blessings unlocked from this act of generosity won't be fathomed until we get to heaven.

Abraham with Melchizedek

Let's look at another example of holy generosity from our forefather of the faith, Abraham. One thing I find fascinating about God is how He uses families and intends for children to go further than their parents in the things of the Lord. It's not in the scope of this book, but as I marvel at Abraham's faithfulness, I wonder if there is a tragedy in his father, Terah. It's purely speculative, but I wonder if Terah was given the same call as Abram (later Abraham) and fell short. If that's the case, the story of Abraham shows even further the goodness of God and His mercy in calling Terah's son.

> Terah took his son Abram, his grandson Lot son of Haran, and his daughter-in-law Sarai, the wife of his son Abram, and together they set out from Ur of the Chaldeans to go to Canaan. But when they came to Harran, they settled there. Terah lived 205 years, and he died in Harran. (Genesis 11:31-32)

Could it be that God called Terah to the land of Canaan, but the worries, cares, comforts, and practicalities of this world held him up in Haran? Perhaps God spoke a similar promise to Terah, but it was not recorded because he wavered in faith and succumbed to unbelief. Let us not be like Terah, staying in the comfort of Haran, but may we press on to the land of Canaan and the fullness of what God has for us!

We are familiar with the story of Abraham. God calls him, transforms him, promises him descendants and blessings as numerous as the stars, and commissions him. Abraham's life was a life of faith, continually looking forward to the fulfillment of God's promises that he himself never lived to fully see. I wonder if he ever truly understood God had an eternal inheritance in mind, much greater than a material, physical family tree. We see his life of faith and call him father, for truly he was the father of the faith.

Now, Abraham, father of the faith, has a remarkable encounter with Melchizedek. During his life, Abraham faced perilous moments, contentious circumstances, barren seasons, and regular fears. Despite all that, he never wavered in his belief in the goodness of God or the Lord's provision. In one instance, after a difficult battle, we see an extraordinary display of generosity. After the battle, Abraham (then Abram) encounters Melchizedek and gives him 10% of the spoils. While we don't know exactly what the spoils entailed, we know that 10% was likely significant.

> After Abram returned from defeating Kedorlaomer and the kings allied with him, the king of Sodom came out to meet him in the Valley of Shaveh (that is, the King's Valley). Then Melchizedek king of Salem brought out bread and wine. He was priest of God Most High, and he blessed Abram, saying, "Blessed be Abram by God Most High, Creator of heaven and earth. And praise be to God Most High, who delivered your enemies into your hand." Then Abram gave him a tenth of everything. (Genesis 14:17-20)

If you're anything like me, that exchange can be quite confusing. Were there priests before the Levitical priesthood Aaron established? Who exactly is Melchizedek, and why did Abraham place him in such high esteem? Fortunately, Hebrews 7:1-10 unpacks this further:

> This Melchizedek was king of Salem and priest of God Most High. He met Abraham returning from the defeat of the kings and blessed him, and Abraham gave him a tenth of everything. First, the name Melchizedek means "king of righteousness"; then also, "king of Salem" means "king of peace." Without father or mother, without genealogy, without beginning of days or end of life, resembling the Son of God, he remains a priest forever. Just think how great he was: Even the patri-

arch Abraham gave him a tenth of the plunder! Now the law requires the descendants of Levi who become priests to collect a tenth from the people—that is, from their fellow Israelites even though they also are descended from Abraham. This man, however, did not trace his descent from Levi, yet he collected a tenth from Abraham and blessed him who had the promises. And without doubt the lesser is blessed by the greater. In the one case, the tenth is collected by people who die; but in the other case, by him who is declared to be living. One might even say that Levi, who collects the tenth, paid the tenth through Abraham, because when Melchizedek met Abraham, Levi was still in the body of his ancestor.

What we see from Abraham is a prophetic act of generosity, a true display of holy generosity. Melchizedek foreshadows the coming messiah, Christ Jesus. Abraham's giving to him is a symbol of reverence toward the greater priesthood that Jesus would embody. This prophetic act toward our coming Messiah and eternal High Priest, who will come and reign forever, rings as a reminder of the blessing we have and the power of prophetically sharing the blessing. In sharing the plunder of battle with Melchizedek, Abraham signifies the power of prophetic generosity as an illustration of Christ's plan for the fulfillment of His promises.

Cornelius the Centurion

Cornelius was an unsaved centurion who feared God. He prayed regularly and generously gave alms to the poor. It is this combination of prayer and giving that so moves the heart of God that He sends an angel to visit Cornelius.

At Caesarea there was a man named Cornelius, a centurion in what was known as the Italian Regiment. He and all his family were devout and God-fearing; he gave generously to those in need and prayed to God regularly. One day at about three in the afternoon he had a vision. He distinctly saw an angel of God, who came to him and said, "Cornelius!" Cornelius stared at him in fear. "What is it, Lord?" he asked. The angel answered, "Your prayers and gifts to the poor have come up as a memorial offering before God. Now send men to Joppa to bring back a man named Simon who is called Peter. He is staying with Simon the tanner, whose house is by the sea." When the angel who spoke to him had gone, Cornelius called two of his servants and a devout soldier who was one of his attendants. He told them everything that had happened and sent them to Joppa. (Acts 10:1-8)

As the story goes, after the angel visits Cornelius and tells him to send men to Peter's exact location to bring him back, Peter himself has a vision. In the vision, Peter is reminded by our Savior, "Do not call anything impure that God has made clean" (Acts 10:15), indicating that Gentiles, too, could share in salvation thanks to Jesus' death on the cross. Peter arrives at Cornelius' house, preaches the gospel, and, while he is still speaking, the Holy Spirit falls on the house and all those invited to hear the message.

While Peter was still speaking these words, the Holy Spirit came on all who heard the message. The circumcised believers who had come with Peter were astonished that the gift of the Holy Spirit had been poured out even on Gentiles. For they heard them speaking in tongues and praising God. Then Peter said, "Surely no one can stand in the way of their being baptized with water. They have received the Holy Spirit just as we have." So he ordered that they be baptized in the name of Jesus Christ. Then they asked Peter to stay with them for a few days. (Acts 10:44-48)

One man's devotion, through giving and prayer, sparked a

revival. The entire congregation, if you will, was saved under Cornelius' roof in one moment. What was at the root of this incredible encounter? As the angel answered, "Your prayers and gifts to the poor have come up as a memorial offering before God." God was so moved by this man's display of generosity that He sent an angel to tell him to send for Peter so he can hear the gospel. God sends two angels in response to this act of holy generosity.

A Poor Widow

Finally, let us look at a poor widow, who offers everything she has —two small copper coins—to the temple treasury. Jesus sees this act of generosity and the heart behind her giving, not the dollar amount. He calls His disciples over to teach them, and all who would follow Him, a lesson:

> Calling his disciples to him, Jesus said, "Truly I tell you, this poor widow has put more into the treasury than all the others. They all gave out of their wealth; but she, out of her poverty, put in everything—all she had to live on." (Mark 12:43-44)

This poor widow shows that a heart fully generous and fully surrendered is an extravagant gift in itself. It's not the size of the gift that moves God's heart; it's the heart behind the gift. I pray that we would be a people who walk in holy generosity and so move the heart of Jesus.

IT'S YOUR TURN

Holy generosity isn't limited to the Old Testament or the heroes of the faith. You and I can participate. Heaven roars in celebration when the children of God catch this vision. What is an area of your life that you can generously sow into the kingdom? What would you do if you knew you could move the heart of God in such a way? God is looking for followers who will trust Him completely. He isn't concerned about the size or type of gift; He's interested in the overflow of the heart. Don't miss an opportunity to move the heart of God through your generosity.

9

WHAT ARE YOU BUILDING?

*I was young and now I am old, yet I have never seen
the righteous forsaken or their children
begging bread. They are always generous and
lend freely; their children will be a blessing.*

PSALM 37:25-26

Picture this. You go to a church that is growing, people are getting saved, and you're seeing fruit. You love it and have met amazing friends who also go there. One Sunday, the pastor takes the stage and announces the church is moving buildings. The current space no longer meets the needs of the church, and it's time to move to something bigger. Something better. You are beyond excited—*it's about time*, you might even think. Then, as the pastor makes this announcement, he shares that the congregation needs to raise money to support the project, as they don't want to neglect the needs of the local community you've been supporting. He asks everyone to prayerfully consider what to give, encouraging each to give whatever the Lord puts on their heart.

The next week, members of the church bring forward their donations. Some are small, but some are quite large. One couple walks to the front of the church and announces they've sold their house and are giving the entirety of their profits to the new building project. You can't believe it. What generosity! But then, something unusual happens. The pastor doesn't look happy. He just received a huge donation—why is he not happy? He says a few words to the couple. Suddenly, something shocking happens. The couple collapses. They are not moving. What happened? The paramedics arrive and declare the couple dead.

It sounds like a bizarre story, but what if I told you that it was —with some creative license and modern liberties—taken straight from the Bible? God did some wild things in the Old Testament, but what if I reminded you this story is from the New Testament? *What!?* Something doesn't compute. I thought God was loving and kind, slow to anger, and abounding in grace. Maybe this sounds too far-fetched to be real. Yet, just as we explored how generosity can move the heart of God, there are also times where radical generosity is not always holy or even pleasing to God. But first, let me share a few examples of building projects stewarded in ways honoring to the Lord.

OBEDIENCE IN THE SLOW PROVISION

Two out of the last three churches I have called home embarked on building projects while I was a regular attendee. The first was my church in Seattle. We met in a school gymnasium in the northern part of the city, close to Seattle Pacific University. When I first moved, it took me a while to find a home church. My friend, Clark, joined me the first time I attended a service. If you've ever looked for a church, you know it can sometimes be difficult to find the right fit. No church is perfect. Sadly, we are all sinful and make up the church, so even if there was a perfect church, the minute you or I showed up, it would become imperfect. I like what my current pastor, Mark, says about church: "Just because you had a bad experience with church once doesn't mean you should stop attending. I've had bad tacos before that gave me food poisoning, but that doesn't mean I stop eating." What an amazing analogy!

I was looking for a church and had probably attended 5-10 different ones by that point. Nothing seemed to be a fit. A friend from back home contacted me through Facebook and recommended a church. I told Clark, so we planned to attend the next Sunday. Since the church met in a gymnasium, the chairs were arranged in almost a U-shape, with the opening to your left, where the pastor and worship team stood. Clark and I sat in the far back left corner, closest to the entry and exit. There were only about a hundred people attending that service, one of two. The pastor, Andrew, gave his sermon, we closed with a song, and then we headed for the door. Neither of us had any intention of socializing with strangers. But when we turned to leave, we found the pastor standing between us and the door, looking directly at us. He wanted to talk.

There are two things about Andrew I grew to love: first, he is incredibly passionate and loves Jesus with his whole heart; and second, he is serious and does not mess around when it comes to obeying God's Word. Clark and I must have caught his attention while he was preaching that Sunday. His serious nature was on full display in this first meeting, as we saw from the intensity on his face; we were not getting out of there without a conversation. We had a short chat, and both Clark and I ended up calling that church home for the next two years. I met incredible friends and developed deep friendships while I was there. Sometimes I wonder, if Andrew had not intentionally sought us out, if I would have ever gone back. I'm sure there's a sermon in there for another time. However, back to the building project.

Andrew announced one Sunday that we were going to move out of the gymnasium and buy a plot of land to build a church so we had a permanent location. We were growing out of the gymnasium and needed more space for what God was asking us to do: lean into the community and create a space for programs during the week that only a permanent location could afford. At the time, I was co-leading a small group, and I remember Andrew showing up to share his vision for the building. Andrew was so bold and direct—I loved it.

My roommate and good friend asked him, "Why are we doing this? Do we even need the space? And what if God doesn't provide?" Andrew's response was simple: "We're doing this because God asked us to do it." The conviction and humility to share that this was not his plan to grow the church, have a better building, or make his life easier, more predictable, or stable—the sole motivation was obedience to the Word of God. I'll never forget that season. Although I anticipated miraculous, rapid provision, that's not what happened. We didn't raise the funds in a moment; there were no major donations. Yet, over the span of eighteen months, we hit milestone after milestone, and slowly but surely, God made a way. We eventually bought land, demolished the current structure, and built a community center and church to reach the community.

FAITH FOR THE IMPOSSIBLE

What is it with me and building projects? I do not know. But as I mentioned, two out of the last three churches I regularly attended embarked on ambitious building plans. The second is entirely the opposite of my first experience. Oceans Church, in Irvine, California, is led by Pastor Mark. What I love about Oceans is the hunger for the presence of God and how it is a church of great faith. Beyond the powerful worship and incredible teachings, the faith Mark instills into our congregation, with a vision to see California restored and the kingdom of heaven come, is inspiring. I still find myself wrestling with the faith that Mark has and feeling convicted that I don't have enough of my own. That's the kind of church I want to go to—not one where I feel comfortable week after week, but one where I feel challenged to grow, rubbed the wrong way because I'm being pruned, and pushed out to step into more.

When my wife and I first started attending Oceans, they were meeting in a tent in a parking lot. This became their practice over COVID. Not only was it for safety, but they simply did not have the space in the current building they were leasing to fit everyone inside. Southern California must be the only place in the country where you can get by with church under a tent year-round. We were attending for about a year and a half when Mark took the stage and made the announcement.

An opportunity opened, and we had the chance to buy a building off-market just down the road from our current location. We were saving to renovate our leased building, but when this opportunity came up, it meant we could have a permanent location. But we had to act fast. Land in Southern California, much like Seattle, is not cheap, and the window before the property would hit the market was narrow. It was $20 million, and we needed to raise the initial deposit of $2 million in two weeks. As a church, we had previously raised around $1.6 million for renovations for the leased property, but we were still $400,000 short with only two weeks to raise the requisite funds for the new property.

I remember that Sunday in the tents when Mark shared the details. As he shared his vision and, ultimately, his plan for the church, those of us in the service prayed while ushers passed around pledge cards for us to fill out the amount we felt called to provide. At the time, my son was just under one year old. He was extremely active (he started walking at ten months, so we spent this morning chasing him around the tents). We watched in awe at the scene unfolding as people responded to the voice of God, pledging all sorts of gifts to contribute to His house.

I had witnessed similar moments when kingdom generosity grips a group of people from my experience at YWAM and my church in NYC. This felt the same. It is truly something to marvel at when the spirit of generosity falls on a church. After collecting all pledges, we concluded the service with a worship song. The next week, Mark shared the news with the church—we raised the $400,000 for the building!

THE DANGER OF PERFORMATIVE GENEROSITY

Whether it is in slow provision or in the faith-filled wonder of radical provision, true giving and freedom are rooted in response to God's Word and obedience paired with faith. As I saw with both my church in Seattle and Oceans Church, whether it's systematic and over the course of time or quick in the matter of weeks, generosity that is Spirit-led and responsive is the type of giving that honors God. He wants surrendered hearts that are fully His, not outward displays of piety.

Now back to our original story. While the previous examples of generosity touch the heart of God, the Bible illustrates a form of unholy generosity.

> Now a man named Ananias, together with his wife Sapphira, also sold a piece of property. With his wife's full knowledge he kept back part of the money for himself, but brought the rest and put it at the apostles' feet. Then Peter said, "Ananias, how is it that Satan has so filled your heart that you have lied to the Holy Spirit and have kept for yourself some of the money you received for the land? Didn't it belong to you before it was sold? And after it was sold, wasn't the money at your disposal? What made you think of doing such a thing? You have not lied just to human beings but to God." When Ananias heard this, he fell down and died. And great fear seized all who heard what had happened. Then some young men came forward, wrapped up his body, and carried him out and buried him. About three hours later his wife came in, not knowing what had happened. Peter asked her, "Tell me, is this the price you and Ananias got for the land?" "Yes," she said, "that is the price." Peter said to her, "How could you conspire to test the Spirit of the Lord? Listen! The feet of the men who buried your husband are at the door, and they will carry you out also." At that moment she fell down at his feet and died. Then the young men came in and, finding her dead, carried her out and buried her

beside her husband. Great fear seized the whole church and all
who heard about these events. (Acts 5:1-11)

Ananias and Sapphira! We may have heard this story before,
but do we understand the gravity of it? Do we understand the
seriousness of lying to the Holy Spirit—outward shows of piety
that are out of alignment with a heart of humility? God does not
delight in sacrifice, but obedience.

> But Samuel replied: "Does the LORD delight in burnt offerings
> and sacrifices as much as in obeying the LORD? To obey is
> better than sacrifice, and to heed is better than the fat of rams."
> (1 Samuel 15:22)

David also understood this, as he so eloquently illuminates in
Psalm 40:6: "Sacrifice and offering you did not desire—but my
ears you have opened—burnt offerings and sin offerings you did
not require."

God does not delight in the sacrifice we are making as much as
He does in our obedience—our opened ears to the voice of God.
He isn't delighted when we give our entire paycheck and feel the
pain of it; He is delighted when we obey! He wants obedient
hearts, not full paychecks! Oh, how we miss the heart of Jesus if
we believe He is impressed with large sums of money and not
with the simple obedience of a child obeying their Father.

It's not the rich with their vast sums of giving who please the
heart of God but the love expressed from a heart that adores the
Maker of heaven and earth.

Ananias and Saphira provide a picture of a spiritual heart
posture. If I look back at my own giving, how many times have I
fallen into the same trap? How many times have I given to receive
praise from man? How many times have I given to impress
pastors? How many times have I given to make myself feel more
holy? How many times have I given as an attempt to earn God's
favor?

Sadly, it's probably more times than I'd like to admit. What about you? How many times have you fallen into the same performative-based, man-pleasing, giving trap as Ananias and Sapphira? May we have hearts that operate out of obedience to our Father's voice, not those seeking to provide an offering that pleases men.

OBEDIENT HEARTS OVER IMPRESSIVE DONATIONS

There was a time I didn't truly understand this principle. My goal was to yearly increase my percentage of the tithe I gave. It became performance-based, as if it were falling back into a duty or obligation like a challenge instead of a delight. Then, one year, the Lord impressed on my heart Psalm 51:16-17.

> You do not delight in sacrifice, or I would bring it; you do not take pleasure in burnt offerings. My sacrifice, O God, is a broken spirit; a broken and contrite heart you, God, will not despise.

God shifted my heart to relationship, surrender, and response to His promptings over percentages, vast sums, and performance. He moved my heart into alignment with His and away from a mathematical equation or calculated risk. He was faithful to love me in my infancy with generosity and used my openness to grow me. Once I surrendered and gave up my desire to "test God," I found greater freedom, greater joy, and greater choice. My obedience paved the way to freedom, and my life of giving moved back into delight as I chose to freely give as a response—not out of obligation.

God is filled with joy when He finds a heart that is fully surrendered—fully broken and made whole in Him, fully assured in Him, fully trusting in Him, fully found in Him, and fully complete in Him alone. This delights God more than any of our offerings and sacrifices. May we be a people with hearts fully surrendered and open to hear His voice, walking in simple obedience to bring joy to our Father in heaven.

10

MAXIMIZING KINGDOM IMPACT

*I will make you into a great nation, and I will bless
you; I will make your name great, and you will
be a blessing.*

GENESIS 12:2

God blesses us to be a blessing. You are the primary vehicle for getting God's Word out and showcasing His goodness to a world in need. And it starts now. On this earth, not in eternity. And it's not someone else's job. It's our privilege to be used by God to advance His kingdom and reflect His glory.

We advance His kingdom as we help others through our time, talents, and treasure. We reflect His glory as we share testimonies of God's provision and goodness—as we surrender our hearts and step out in faith. In each of these small, obedient decisions, we shape our kingdom legacy, our kingdom impact. The type of legacy we leave behind, the type of legacy we sow into, is shaped by our actions here and now.

God wants to use our generosity to maximize His impact. It's a true partnership to get the gospel message to the nations. And here's the key: it all comes from a place of humility. God is looking for humble hearts He can use to make an impact. It's His impact—not ours. We simply partner with Him through our generosity, which also allows us to impact our families, neighborhoods, churches, and, in turn, nations.

The great thing is that, because God is in it, He will multiply what we surrender and make it even more beautiful, meaningful, and impactful. Just as the boy with the two small fish and five small barley loaves brought his simple offering to Jesus and watched it feed a multitude (John 6:8-13), the simplest offering, when brought to Jesus, makes an impact far surpassing our expectations. In the same way, the woman who poured out her alabaster jar of costly perfume at the feet of Jesus left behind a legacy of generosity captured in the Gospels we previously explored. Whether with loaves and fish or with perfume, both show us this truth: our acts of generosity, no matter how small, can create a lasting legacy.

We are called to be the thermostat in a world that is lost. We have the keys to the kingdom and can change the temperature of a room when we walk in it with faith, hope, and love. As Jesus continually outpours into our lives, and we activate it through our generosity, we find that this outpouring continues in abundance despite our perpetual outflow. God wants to use your sphere of influence for kingdom impact. Whether it's neighborhoods or nations, close relationships or church, God wants to shine His light through you.

NEIGHBORHOODS

After we moved, our new neighbors across the street quickly became some of our best friends—well, Wess' best friends. Emma and I like to refer to them as "Wess' adopted grandparents." Wess loves going over there to jump off their little ledge and say hello. It feels like we live in the 1950s because, though he's only two years old, Wess wants to go over to "see what Mr. Harvey and Ms. Donna are doing." To him, they have a fun house because Ms. Donna has a lemon tree that she lets Wess help cut and a pool he can swim in. Harvey and Donna treat Wess so well, and we were so grateful for good neighbors that we made cookies for them during our first Christmas living here. Our first spring, Donna had Wess come over and help cut the lemon tree, giving us a lemon in return. After receiving a few lemons, Emma made lemon scones for Harvey and Donna as a thank you.

We often walk over and talk regularly, spending time with Harvey and Donna in the rhythm of life. More than just saying hi, we swing by for a few minutes, or they come over to our yard. We met some other neighbors as well and began saying hi. Emma and I knew we were called to this house but weren't entirely sure why. We prayed for God's kingdom to come to our neighborhood as it is in heaven. One night when I was praying, the Lord revealed how He was bringing His kingdom to our street. It wasn't in a big glamorous way. It wasn't in mass salvations or baptisms. It was in the simple generosity of sharing cookies and inspiring their generosity of sharing lemons, time, and life.

God showed me that when His kingdom comes, it doesn't mean everyone is immediately saved. It's more intangible, more spiritual. The evidence of the kingdom is in our midst (Luke 17:20-21). It's in our day-to-day. We carry the kingdom with us and advance it through our loving actions. We make kingdom impact as we live our lives generously—not through the big acts only but through small acts of kindness and generosity. We are light to our neighborhoods, to a world that desperately needs it. As simple an act as making cookies and saying hello can have an impact on our neighborhoods. The Lord revealed to me that we are bringing the kingdom to our neighborhood through our relationships. Our impact is so much more than we realize when we walk with Jesus and let the world see Him through us.

NATIONS

During my time with YWAM, I joined a small team of ten on a mission trip to Thailand. One of our stops was in Chiang Mai, where we helped host a Christian business conference. We offered our time and talents by volunteering on the audiovisual team and greeting guests.

During one of the conference breaks, a few of us visited a nearby mall. While in the country, we made every effort to learn as much Thai as possible so we could connect with people, pray with them, and offer encouragement. In the mall, a man named Nun approached three of us and asked if we would sign a petition he was working on. Immediately, we saw this as an opportunity to minister to him. After a short conversation, we asked if he had any pain in his body we could pray for. I often find that physical pain can open the door for ministry, as offering prayer for healing demonstrates God's care in a tangible way. Nun shared that he had pain in his back and was open to prayer. I'll never forget what happened next.

The three of us laid hands on him and prayed. As I prayed, I felt chills run through my body. When I finished, Nun opened his eyes, looked at me, and asked, "What did you do to me?" He explained that he felt power run down his back and the pain was completely gone. God healed him. We shared with him how good our God is and that it was Jesus who had healed his back. We ministered to him further but soon had to leave to continue sight-seeing and evangelism in other parts of town. To our surprise, Nun asked if he could come with us. He was so captivated by the goodness of God and the miracle he experienced that he wanted to learn more about Jesus—and even join us in sharing the gospel.

For the rest of that day, Nun traveled with us as we evangelized in the streets. He jumped in to translate when needed, and we continued to encourage him and help him process what God did in his life. In a single encounter at a mall in Chiang Mai,

Nun's life was forever changed. He experienced the personal love of Jesus in a tangible way.

All we did was offer our time, and God used it to reach a man in Thailand who now carries a testimony of His goodness. I love the biblical comparison that Joshua was the son of Nun. In the same way, I pray Nun would father a "Joshua" generation in Thailand—children who walk in the light of Jesus and lead their nation closer to God's promised kingdom. May Nun's life and family become a lasting testimony of Christ's love and power in Thailand!

RELATIONSHIPS

More than moving in our neighborhoods and nations, God wants to move in and through your life to impact the relationships you have with others for His kingdom. He wants to bring the light of Jesus to your family, coworkers, siblings, friends, and acquaintances. One way He does this is by making us interruptible.

The Bible uses two different Greek words for time—*chronos* and *kairos*. *Chronos* refers to the chronological nature of time, whereas *kairos* refers to the impromptu, appointed, special, or opportune moments. We see an example of one of these kairos moments when Jesus is interrupted by the woman with the issue of blood. Jesus is walking through a crowd when a woman touches the hem of His garment, believing if she does so she will be healed. After touching His garment, Jesus realizes power has gone out from Him and looks to see who touched Him. Amazed, the disciples ask, "What do you mean, 'Who touched you?' You're surrounded by people." But Jesus knows differently. He sees the woman, stops, speaks with her, and forgives her sins. The amazing thing about this story is that Jesus was on His way to raise a young girl from the dead when this happened.

Jesus was never so caught up in the destination that he wasn't open to those special interruptible moments. His time was something He owned; it didn't own Him. We see evidence of this throughout His life. From rebuking the disciples who tried preventing children from coming to Him (Matthew 19:14) to performing His first miracle of turning water into wine (John 2:4), Jesus always made Himself available, always open to being interrupted.

My friend Kris recently shared a powerful kairos story with me. While working out of a coffee shop in Kona, a man walked in and asked if there was a prayer room on the YWAM base nearby. Though Kris was admittedly a little annoyed by the interruption, a simple question opened the door to a two-hour conversation.

As they talked, Kris shared his heart for bringing the gospel to the nations as a full-time missionary. He soon learned this man was a successful businessman. At the end of their conversation, he asked if Kris had a family website where he could give. Kris explained that he had just deactivated it, not wanting to pay the $200 annual fee to keep it running. Undeterred, the man asked if there was another way to give right then and there. He told Kris to open his computer and donated $10,000 to support Kris and his family on the spot.

This is just one of many stories Kris carries of God's provision through the radical generosity of others. What struck me most is how it all began—not with strategy or fundraising techniques but with Kris making time for the people around him. A simple interruption turned into divine provision.

If I look at my own life, I don't think I can always say the same —that I'm interruptible and available for these kairos moments. What about you? Are you interruptible, or are you too busy for people? Is your time so occupied, so planned out, that you neglect the needs of those around you? Are you available when a friend just needs to talk? Are you able to pause when a child or spouse wants undivided attention? Are you available to volunteer at church and fill a need?

Or even further, are you generous with forgiveness? This is an area that's truly a struggle! To those who have hurt me in the past, wronged me, or mistreated me, am I generous with forgiveness? If I answer honestly, the answer many times is no. To forgive is one of the most difficult things we are called to do as followers of Christ. However, the Bible tells us we are to forgive. In his letter to the church at Ephesus, the apostle Paul instructs the believers, "Be kind and compassionate to one another, forgiving each other, just as in Christ God forgave you" (Ephesians 4:32).

The Bible calls us to forgive to the level Christ forgave us! Oh, what generosity; it is truly unmatchable. Christ forgave us so much that He literally left the perfection of heaven to come to earth in the form of man, humbling Himself to the point of death on a cross, so we might be forgiven of our sins. Truly, as His servants, if Christ made such a sacrifice, we too are called to be generous with our forgiveness (seventy times seven according to Matthew 18:22). May we look for opportunities to invite Jesus into our relationships through divine interruptions.

CHURCH

God wants us to be generous toward the body of Christ—His bride. Christ loved the church so much, He died for it (Ephesians 5:25). If we are to look and love like Christ, we must love the things He loves, chief of which are people and the church. My grandfather, who recently passed away, embodied this better than anyone I know. He dedicated his life to serving Christ.

From his time serving in the Air Force hosting a Bible study for service members to his over sixty years serving in his church as a worship pastor and later on the pastoral care team, my grandpa worked tirelessly to serve. If you spent any amount of time speaking with him, you quickly heard him bragging about the church. Its happenings were always on the tip of his tongue, along with how blessed he was by God and how grateful he was for his family. Working for little accolade and rarely ever preaching—save for a handful of times—my grandpa lived his life for the church. Whenever a member was in the hospital or had a loved one in need, he was always available, always offering his time.

One story in particular stands out that I learned after his passing. A few years back, a church member was in the hospital for back surgery. My grandpa stayed with his wife in the waiting room for the entire eight-hour surgery even though it was his birthday. The woman he waited with later posted on Facebook how grateful she was for his company in her time of need.

Truly, he loved the church as Christ loved the church. How do you mirror Christ's love for His bride? Do you speak well of it? Do you freely give your time, talents, and finances? God created us to play a part in advancing His kingdom in partnership with the church. I pray we may have eyes to see the church as Christ saw the church—a bride worth loving with everything we have.

God wants to use you to impact your entire sphere of influence. Though you may not cross borders into nations, we all have a part to play in our relationships, churches, and neighborhoods. From the simple acts of generosity to the giving of our time, Christ created you to make a positive impact for His kingdom.

One of my favorite parts of giving financially is how we can partner with those who have dedicated their lives to serving Christ and share in their inheritance. As a unified body of Christ, maybe like me, you work full-time and don't have access to go on mission trips to the nations. What I love is that we can give to those who do and share in their efforts by financing trips. In doing so, we participate in the Great Commission from afar while still having opportunities to be generous with our time in our neighborhood and churches.

As we provide generously to advance the gospel, we labor with Christ and with those on the front lines. Each of us stewards whatever is in our hands to collectively advance God's kingdom. When we bring what we have to the feet of Jesus, we see He multiplies our generosity for a greater impact than we could have imagined (or accomplished on our own). Much like the little boy who brought his lunch to Jesus only to witness Him multiply the loaves and fishes to feed more than 5,000 people (John 6:8-13), we too, as we bring what we have to Him, can watch amazed as the impact extends to multitudes.

What are practical ways you can advance the kingdom of heaven in your sphere of influence? Are there people you can bless financially? What time and talents can you give? Where can you begin using generosity to impact the kingdom?

11

THE ABUNDANT LIFE

*And my God will meet all your needs according to
the riches of his glory in Christ Jesus.*

PHILIPPIANS 4:19

Walking in kingdom generosity doesn't just bless the recipient of
our generosity—we also benefit. As we look outward to make a
kingdom impact with the use of our time, talents, and treasures in
our relationships, neighborhoods, churches, and nations, we
receive rewards this side of eternity. These rewards shape the
abundant life Jesus speaks of in John 10:10.

It's almost as if God, fully aware of humanity's innate desire
for instant gratification and earthly tendencies, clearly outlines the
rewards He offers to His devoted followers as an encouragement
to continue along the path of righteousness. Scripture spells out
these benefits and rewards for those who follow Him—promises
available here and now to strengthen us as we live for His kingdom. They are unlocked by our generosity and faithful obedience
to our Father in heaven. How amazing is it that God literally gives
us the Bible as an owner's manual for how to live the best possible
life—now *and* in heaven?!

My son is two years old and has a strong personality. He knows what he wants and when he wants it. The Lord showed me recently that Emma and I, as parents, must teach him to listen well so he learns obedience and will one day obey Jesus' words. If we don't set the foundation now, he won't learn submission to authority, and I don't want him to live his life for himself. I want him to live surrendered to Jesus—obedient to God's words.

To help him learn, my wife had the brilliant idea to create a listening chart. She drew a table using markers on a blank piece of paper with three boxes across. Each time he listens when we ask him to do something, he adds a sticker to one of the boxes. When the boxes across the row are filled, he receives a special treat, like a handful of chocolate chips or a new toy. When he doesn't listen, we put a toy away that he can earn back through his "good listening." The incentive of seeing the boxes visually filled with stickers works amazingly. He loves it so much that now he asks for new tasks so he can listen and obey to fill the chart.

Jesus tells us we are to become like children if we are to enter the kingdom of heaven (Matthew 18:3). The visualization of the reward for Wess through the listening chart helps him make the right decision and focus on obedience. Similarly, the Bible lays out the rewards we are entitled to for our obedience—our faithful acts of service and generosity. It's important for us to know the benefits God provides so we can remind ourselves of why we step out in generosity. God clearly lays these out as both earthly rewards and benefits. His benefits are described in Psalm 103:1–5.

> Praise the LORD, my soul; all my inmost being, praise his holy name. Praise the LORD, my soul, and forget not all his benefits —who forgives all your sins and heals all your diseases, who redeems your life from the pit and crowns you with love and compassion, who satisfies your desires with good things so that your youth is renewed like the eagle's.

To the faithful follower, the Lord provides forgiveness,

restored health, deliverance, redemption, love, satisfaction, and renewed energy. What an amazing benefits package Jesus offers His followers! It blows away any compensation package we will ever be offered for our vocational work. Though generosity and faithfulness may stretch, shake, and send us out of our comfort zone, we are provided everything we need for our souls to be satisfied. Let us remind our spirit of the benefits our Lord graciously provides. Certainly, His yoke is easy, and His burden is light.

Instead of letting ourselves be caught in the trap of stress, anxiety, fear, doubt, or worry, we should rather lift up our spirits and set our gaze upon the Lord on His high hill. I find myself regularly needing to speak to my soul. Even as I write this section, anxiety and fear crouch at the door, but I choose to speak to my soul, refresh myself in the Lord, and offer my anxieties to Him (Psalm 42:5).

When we lift our gaze to Jesus and speak to our soul, we remind ourselves of the Lord's benefits and the blessings we have in Him. And, as we renew our energy, we can remind ourselves of why we choose to faithfully obey His Word and walk in kingdom generosity—because He first loved us! And as we walk in this love, we share light with a world in need. We love others, bless others, comfort others, and encourage others. As we do, we please our Father in heaven and experience His rewards. Let's take a look at these rewards more closely.

PROSPERITY AND BLESSING

Now it shall come to pass, if you diligently obey the voice of the LORD your God, to observe carefully all His commandments which I command you today, that the LORD your God will set you high above all nations of the earth. And all these blessings shall come upon you and overtake you, because you obey the voice of the LORD your God. (Deuteronomy 28:1-2 NKJV)

The Lord promises prosperity and blessings for His covenant people—those who carefully obey His commands. The Holman Study Bible notes, "Moses promised that the blessings for covenant obedience would not merely lie at hand passively, but with dynamic life and power would overtake the obedient person. There is no escaping the blessings and favor of the Lord when a person is careful to obey him."*

How I love that! Our faithful obedience cannot escape the blessings of the Lord. In my life, I've seen this radical takeover of blessing. It's like trying to outrun an avalanche—eventually, your faithful obedience results in a surge of blessing so great you can't avoid it. In my career, I was promoted three times in six years, increasing my income rapidly. God's promises for covenant obedience aren't theoretical—they're real and relevant today.

PERFECT PEACE

You will keep in perfect peace those whose minds are steadfast, because they trust in you. (Isaiah 26:3)

I have told you these things, so that in me you may have peace. In this world you will have trouble. But take heart! I have overcome the world. (John 16:33)

In some of the most difficult seasons of my life—times of loneliness, stress, and uncertainty—I found peace when I refreshed myself in the Lord. During a three-month period of unemployment, even though it was frustrating, I had a deep, unshakable confidence God was perfectly orchestrating everything behind the scenes. When I was lonely, God provided divine friendships to help me feel loved and supported, though my family was distant.

---

* Holman Bible Publishers. (2013). Deuteronomy 28:1-2 (p. 317).

SLEEP

In peace I will lie down and sleep, for you alone, LORD, make me dwell in safety. (Psalm 4:8)

When you lie down, you will not be afraid; when you lie down, your sleep will be sweet. (Proverbs 3:24)

In vain you rise early and stay up late, toiling for food to eat—for he grants sleep to those he loves. (Psalm 127:2)

Nightmares, sleeplessness, and insomnia don't have to be the norm for believers. We are overcomers. We can claim these promises over our lives and rest in His peace, knowing that restful sleep is part of His design and provision.

REST

Come to me, all you who are weary and burdened, and I will give you rest. Take my yoke upon you and learn from me, for I am gentle and humble in heart, and you will find rest for your souls. (Matthew 11:28-29)

I've made it a habit to rest on Sundays and avoid overscheduling my time. While sleep refers to the physical act, rest is more of an emotional, spiritual state of avoiding busyness and choosing to create space with your time. Several times, I considered taking on a second job to earn more, but God clearly showed me He could provide more through rest and faithfulness where I was already planted. And He sure did! Especially in times of financial stress, we must be careful to avoid striving to achieve something that only God can provide. This is where our active trust in God shows itself to be refined—choosing to accept His gift of rest while allowing Him to be our ultimate provider.

LONG LIFE

> Honor your father and mother—which is the first commandment with a promise—so that it may go well with you and that you may enjoy long life on the earth. (Ephesians 6:2-3)

This is a promise I've seen come to life in my own family. Two of my grandparents recently turned ninety years old, and my wife, Emma, has a great-grandmother who lived to be one hundred and one years old!

CHILDREN

> Children are a heritage from the LORD, offspring a reward from him. (Psalm 127:3)

When Emma and I prayed about starting a family, I wrestled with the decision. We were enjoying our freedom—surfing, traveling, and eating out. But in prayer, the Lord whispered, "I have the greatest blessing waiting for you." At one point, we prayed for a Tesla because we thought it would be such a blessing to have an electric car. But God spoke again about starting a family, "If someone offered you a brand-new Tesla, when would you want it?" The answer was obvious: now. That clarity helped us move forward, and nine months later, we welcomed Wess into the world —far better than any Tesla!

PROVISION

> But blessed is the one who trusts in the LORD, whose confidence is in him. They will be like a tree planted by the water that sends out its roots by the stream. It does not fear when heat

comes; its leaves are always green. It has no worries in a year of drought and never fails to bear fruit. (Jeremiah 17:7-8)

Look at the birds of the air; they do not sow or reap or store away in barns, and yet your heavenly Father feeds them. Are you not much more valuable than they? (Matthew 6:26)

So do not worry, saying, "What shall we eat?" or "What shall we drink?" or "What shall we wear?" For the pagans run after all these things, and your heavenly Father knows that you need them. (Matthew 6:31-32)

God promises to provide for all our needs. These include our physical needs (food, shelter, water, and clothing), our relational needs, and most importantly, our spiritual needs. God's provision is not limited to simply financial blessings. He wants us to be whole and complete in all areas of our lives, lacking nothing. Our simple acts of obedience unlock this blessing of provision across multiple dimensions of our being. Though at times our definition of provision may differ from God's, we can rest assured—we will never lack.

STABILITY

Cast your cares on the LORD and he will sustain you; he will never let the righteous be shaken. (Psalm 55:22)

This verse is one of my favorites. I memorized it and repeat it often, especially during uncertain seasons. It always anchors me. Storms of life are bound to come, but faithful followers of Jesus are promised they will not be shaken by these storms. More than what to do with our anxiety—*bringing it to Jesus*—this verse promises believers that they can be unmovable, unshakeable by choosing to stay rooted in

Him. In the Pacific Northwest there are some of the most magnificent redwood trees. Not only do they grow tall and their roots grow deep, but they are also immoveable when the winds and rains fall during winter seasons. I imagine we believers are like a group of these giant redwoods as we hold tightly to this promise.

GOD'S FAVOR (IN WORK)

Those who work their land will have abundant food, but those who chase fantasies have no sense. (Proverbs 12:11)

You will eat the fruit of your labor; blessings and prosperity will be yours. (Psalm 128:2)

Just as Joseph worked hard and found favor with Potiphar, David worked hard and found favor with King Saul, and Daniel worked hard and found favor with King Nebuchadnezzar, God wants His children to be diligent workers, promising to provide His favor in return. Throughout my career, I've seen the Lord's favor. I've been promoted four times by four different managers over ten years, met and exceeded my goals, and experienced favor with coworkers and leadership—God's hand was evident.

VICTORY OVER ENEMIES

The LORD will grant that the enemies who rise up against you will be defeated before you. They will come at you from one direction but flee from you in seven. (Deuteronomy 28:7)

God has won the ultimate victory through His death on the cross, and now we can have confidence that we too can overcome. And here's the best part: God fights for us! In fact, one of the Hebrew names for God is Jehovah Nissi, which means "the Lord is our banner," referring to victory. How cool is it that victory is literally found in the name of our King!

A BOOMERANG OF BLESSINGS

Throughout Scripture, we see examples of God's benefits for those who trust in the Lord and follow His ways. In the turbulent times life may bring, believers can rest in these promises of God. Though we step in generosity intending to bless others, God promises that blessings will return to us, allowing us to experience life abundantly.

One Christmas, I bought my brother a boomerang. We went to the park by our house and practiced throwing it for hours. After we learned the technique and threw it at just the right angle, the boomerang came right back to us every time. I like to imagine the earthly rewards promised in the Bible like that boomerang. As we faithfully obey the Word of God, step out in faith, and diligently and generously offer our time, talents, and treasures, the blessings of God—the abundant life—are unlocked in our own lives. These blessings overwhelm us and transform every part of our lives—they truly are the result of an overflowing life of generosity.

The abundant life is an adventure with Jesus—a journey to our true purpose where we can make a kingdom impact and experience the fullness of the Lord's blessings. This is what the Lord had in mind when He spoke of the abundant life. As the ultimate fulfillment of the best possible life, Jesus came so we might live fully dependent on Him, aware of His blessings, and fully satisfied in Him.

WELCOME TO THE ABUNDANT LIFE!

12

ETERNAL INVESTMENTS

*God "will repay each person according to what they
have done."*

ROMANS 2:6

We were all created to live eternally. One of my biggest pet peeves
is the phrase "you only live once." Not simply because it usually
encourages people to do something they'll regret but because we
know biblically it's bad theology! What the Bible teaches is exactly
the opposite; everyone lives twice! We live once on this earth—our
short time equivalent to a tryout or audition—and then forever in
heaven with Christ or eternally separated from Him. Eternity is
very real. Our second life is very real. Our existence will never end.
We will spend unending minutes, hours, and days either with our
heavenly Father and King Jesus in heaven or in the lake of fire.

> Then I saw "a new heaven and a new earth," for the first heaven
> and the first earth had passed away, and there was no longer any
> sea. (Revelation 21:1)

Anyone whose name was not found written in the book of life was thrown into the lake of fire. (Revelation 20:15)

Surrounded by a great cloud of witnesses—those saints who have gone before us and whose lives testify to God's enduring faithfulness—we press on, seeking to make the most of the time entrusted to us on earth (Hebrews 12:1). With longing hearts, we await the grand reunion: the marriage supper of the Lamb at the culmination of all things (Revelation 19:6–9). The Lord, in His great patience, continues to gather His people from every tribe, nation, and tongue until heaven is filled with the fullness of His redeemed (Revelation 7:9).

The book of Revelation is one of my favorites to study. In addition to the apocalyptic imagery and eschatology, the revelation of Jesus' heart for His church and humanity and impending victory spur me on with renewed energy and passion as I study. Understood best as the revelation of Jesus, our Lamb, Victor, Messiah, and King, Revelation draws powerful imagery and symbolic messaging that can't fully be comprehended. But one thing is clear as we study Revelation and other references to heaven and eternity throughout the Bible: eternal rewards are available to each of us. Paul, in his preaching and teaching, spoke of end times regularly (2 Thessalonians 2:5). The second coming of Christ wasn't meant to be entirely mystical but digestible. Paul shared this with the church at Thessalonica, and we can draw from the same well of truth today.

As we explored in the previous chapter, the blessings that come from our kingdom generosity have an impact on our quality of life here on this earth and unlock an abundant life. However, the rewards for our generosity don't stop there. God promises eternal rewards as well. Lasting forever, these rewards never perish, spoil, or fade (Matthew 6:19-21). These rewards are not abstract ideas—they're real, meaningful, and based on how we steward our lives.

The Bible mentions several types of eternal rewards, including crowns, which are given based on our faithfulness, obedience, and endurance. In addition, Scripture teaches that faithful followers of Jesus will be rewarded with positions of authority in His future kingdom. Our level of responsibility in the next life is directly proportional to our trustworthiness in and stewardship of this one.

Jesus shares this principle in Luke 19:17: "'Well done, my good servant!' his master replied. 'Because you have been trustworthy in a very small matter, take charge of ten cities.'"

Our faithfulness on earth qualifies us for roles in governing and executing God's rule during the millennial kingdom and beyond. Let's take a closer look at what Scripture says about the specific eternal rewards awaiting believers, starting with the four crowns.

CROWN OF RIGHTEOUSNESS

Now there is in store for me the crown of righteousness, which the Lord, the righteous Judge, will award to me on that day— and not only to me, but also to all who have longed for his appearing. (2 Timothy 4:8)

Righteousness refers to *right living* and is obtained through our faithful obedience to the Word of God. By walking in right relationship with God, grounded in our faith in Jesus, we live righteously. Everyone who eagerly awaits the Lord's appearing and lives a righteous life will receive the crown of righteousness.

CROWN OF GLORY

To the elders among you, I appeal as a fellow elder and a witness of Christ's sufferings who also will share in the glory to be revealed: Be shepherds of God's flock that is under your care, watching over them—not because you must, but because you are willing, as God wants you to be; not pursuing dishonest gain, but eager to serve; not lording it over those entrusted to you, but being examples to the flock. And when the Chief Shepherd appears, you will receive the crown of glory that will never fade away. (1 Peter 5:1-4)

Faithful leaders, such as pastors and elders, will receive the crown of glory. Those who serve the Church and shepherd God's people well, in accordance with His Word, receive this crown for their service.

CROWN OF LIFE (VICTOR'S CROWN)

Blessed is the one who perseveres under trial because, having stood the test, that person will receive the crown of life that the Lord has promised to those who love him. (James 1:12)

Do not be afraid of what you are about to suffer. I tell you, the devil will put some of you in prison to test you, and you will suffer persecution for ten days. Be faithful, even to the point of death, and I will give you life as your victor's crown. (Revelation 2:10)

The crown of life, or victor's crown, is awarded to those who endure trials, sufferings, and temptations. It appears to be for martyrs—those who died for their faith. He or she who did not love their life so much as to shrink from death for the name of Jesus will receive the crown of life, or the victor's crown, as Revelation calls it.

INCORRUPTIBLE CROWN

Everyone who competes in the games goes into strict training.

They do it to get a crown that will not last, but we do it to get a crown that will last forever. (1 Corinthians 9:25)

This crown is for those who live a disciplined and self-controlled life, striving for spiritual excellence. Just as some train for temporary things, we spend our lives training for eternity, developing spiritual fruit that lasts beyond this life.

Likely the highest honor we can receive, crowns signify one's royal heritage and position in Jesus' kingdom. These crowns are placed before the feet of Jesus and His throne when we worship Him as a sign of our gratitude and devotion to our King (Revelation 4:10-11). For those of us in the Western world, it's difficult to grasp the authority and total power of a monarchy or the full symbolism of a crown. A crown reflects power, authority, law, and judgement. On this side of heaven, these crowns, while known, cannot be understood in full, and their role in executing a heavenly government is temporarily obfuscated. As we graduate from this life, the importance of the crowns will be made clear. Though crowns are likely our chief reward upon entry into heaven and last eternally, the Bible specifies additional rewards for following the way of Christ.

ETERNAL LIFE

For God so loved the world that he gave his one and only Son, that whoever believes in him shall not perish but have eternal life. (John 3:16)

What a blessing we must remember: everyone lives twice, but only some live forever in His presence.

A PLACE IN THE FATHER'S HOUSE

> My Father's house has many rooms; if that were not so, would I
> have told you that I am going there to prepare a place for
> you? And if I go and prepare a place for you, I will come
> back and take you to be with me that you also may be where I
> am. (John 14:2-3)

When my sister invited her coworker to church and she gave her
life to Jesus, I joked that she'll have more square footage in heaven.
Maybe it's true!

INHERITANCE IN GOD'S KINGDOM

> Praise be to the God and Father of our Lord Jesus Christ! In his
> great mercy he has given us new birth into a living hope through
> the resurrection of Jesus Christ from the dead, and into an
> inheritance that can never perish, spoil or fade. This inheritance
> is kept in heaven for you, who through faith are shielded by
> God's power until the coming of the salvation that is ready to be
> revealed in the last time. (1 Peter 1:3-5)

Just as royal heirs receive inheritances from earthly monarchs, we
too, as sons and daughters of the King, receive an eternal inheritance from God.

HEAVENLY TREASURES

> But store up for yourselves treasures in heaven, where moths and
> vermin do not destroy, and where thieves do not break in and
> steal. (Matthew 6:20)

And if anyone gives even a cup of cold water to one of these little ones who is my disciple, truly I tell you, that person will certainly not lose their reward. (Matthew 10:42)

Look, I am coming soon! My reward is with me, and I will give to each person according to what they have done. (Revelation 22:12)

I love walking by Dana Point Harbor and looking at the yachts. As beautiful as they are, they require constant maintenance. But our heavenly treasure? No rust, no rot—just eternal reward, perfectly preserved by the Lord.

HIDDEN MANNA AND A NEW NAME

Whoever has ears, let them hear what the Spirit says to the churches. To the one who is victorious, I will give some of the hidden manna. I will also give that person a white stone with a new name written on it, known only to the one who receives it. (Revelation 2:17)

Just as the Hebrews were sustained by manna in the wilderness, we will also partake in the hidden manna. And just like Abram became Abraham, Sarai became Sarah, Jacob became Israel, Simon became Peter, and Saul became Paul, we'll receive new names in heaven that perfectly reflect our redeemed identity and eternal purpose.

AUTHORITY TO RULE WITH CHRIST

To the one who is victorious, I will give the right to sit with me on my throne, just as I was victorious and sat down with my Father on his throne. (Revelation 3:21)

> "Well done, my good servant!" his master replied. "Because you have been trustworthy in a very small matter, take charge of ten cities." (Luke 19:17)

We won't just be *with* Christ—we will *reign* with Him. I imagine there will be heavenly mayors, governors, and all sorts of leadership roles. The way we steward our current lives qualifies us for these future responsibilities.

RIGHT TO EAT FROM THE TREE OF LIFE

> Whoever has ears, let them hear what the Spirit says to the churches. To the one who is victorious, I will give the right to eat from the tree of life, which is in the paradise of God. (Revelation 2:7)

> Then the angel showed me the river of the water of life, as clear as crystal, flowing from the throne of God and of the Lamb down the middle of the great street of the city. On each side of the river stood the tree of life, bearing twelve crops of fruit, yielding its fruit every month. And the leaves of the tree are for the healing of the nations. (Revelation 22:1-2)

How lovely must the fruit of the tree be that provides life, healing, redemption, and restoration.

A MODEL OF ETERNAL INVESTMENT

About five months after Wess was born, Emma submitted a few pictures of him to a modeling agency. The agency liked him and brought him on. We were both surprised by how much work he got! In a relatively short time, he modeled for Walmart, New Balance, Munchkin, and Disney—even shooting an NFL Shop commercial with Emma. He was a natural and genuinely loved the camera. Entertainment was a new world for me, but Emma had some experience. I had no idea what to think, but we agreed we would continue with his modeling as long as he was having fun.

Emma plays an active role on set, often bringing along toys, stuffed animals, or whatever might help capture the shot the producer is hoping for. As Wess has gotten older, he especially enjoys the snacks and playtime that come with each shoot. Before his most recent job, Emma gently reminded him he never has to do anything he's uncomfortable with—no matter who's asking. When the producer asked if he wanted to ride a bike, he confidently responded, "I don't have to do that." It wasn't quite the situation we anticipated, but we're learning as we go, and we're grateful he already has the courage to speak up for himself.

In order to model, we had to apply for a work permit for Wess and set up a trust fund. The fact he has a trust fund is something Emma and I both laugh at, given our humble backgrounds. Both of my parents were teachers, while Emma's dad worked at a camp and her mom stayed home with the kids. Trust funds were the last thing either of us thought we'd ever learn about.

We set it up and began collecting paychecks for his work. A percentage of the money he earns goes into his trust fund, while the rest goes into a bank account we set up for him. I have a great picture on my phone of Wess as an eight-month-old bringing a check to the bank to deposit.

The more I study eternal rewards, the more I see parallels between Wess' modeling and our lives as followers of Christ. Wess gets selected for a job (or responds to a casting call), shows up to the set, performs what is asked of him, and then receives compensation for his work. Though he's now only two, he has already earned a decent chunk of money. Emma and I manage his finances on his behalf, and I've invested most of his earnings into mutual funds that will hopefully grow and multiply by the time he's old enough to access them.

As a two-year-old, Wess has no comprehension of money.

Even in pretend play, he gives things away freely, has no concept of cost, and doesn't understand that money is required to buy toys. If we gave him the money he earned now, he wouldn't even be able to spend it.

How similar this is to our life in Christ and our eternal rewards. We respond to the prompting of the Holy Spirit (job selection), obey what God asks (show up to the set), continue faithfully (perform our work), and in the end, Christ generously blesses us with eternal rewards (compensation). Just as Wess earns money now that he won't use until later, we earn eternal rewards in this life that we won't fully realize until the next. When Wess turns eighteen, the compounded interest on his earnings will be far greater than anything he receives today—just like our heavenly rewards will make more sense and carry more weight in eternity.

As we live lives marked by radical obedience, generosity, and trust in God's Word, it's essential to maintain an eternal perspective. The rewards of this life, though wonderful, pale in comparison to those awaiting us. Our heavenly rewards are real. They are tangible. They are eternal.

Jesus doesn't just give us His presence—though this alone would be enough. He elevates us to heavenly places and allows us to bring heaven to earth. We receive earthly rewards while partnering with Him now to establish our heavenly lifestyle. He crowns us. He names us. He entrusts us with heavenly authority and fills our storehouses with treasures that never fade. Let us fix our eyes on Him—not only for who He is, but for the glorious kingdom He is preparing for those who love Him.

I pray that we may have eyes to see and ears to hear the things God has in store for those who love Him: "However, as it is written: 'What no eye has seen, what no ear has heard, and what no human mind has conceived'—the things God has prepared for those who love him" (1 Corinthians 2:9).

EPILOGUE: MARANATHA

Grace to all who love our Lord Jesus Christ with an undying love.

EPHESIANS 6:24

Our time on earth is so short. We are not guaranteed tomorrow, but we are guaranteed eternity. Where we spend eternity depends on the choices we make in this life. Do we choose to love Jesus, live for Him, surrender to His will, obey His laws, give generously, and live radically, or do we choose to pursue our own desires? James 4:14 captures the fleeting nature of this life: "Why, you do not even know what will happen tomorrow. What is your life? You are a mist that appears for a little while and then vanishes."

A few years ago, before COVID, I was traveling regularly for work and spent a lot of time in airports. Airports are funny places. They never seem to have what you want—like a gym or a spa—but always have plenty of what no one needs: unhealthy food and duty-free stores. One day, as I sat in the airport, the Holy Spirit gave me a revelation. He spoke to my heart, showing me how this life is like our time spent in an airport. They are simply holdover locations as we await our final destination.

When I'm in an airport, though I'm uncomfortable, I don't spend too much time struggling to rearrange chairs or find the coziest place to relax. I don't look to fill my stomach with Michelin-rated meals. I don't worry about what I wear, and I'm not concerned with gathering more belongings because I only have my suitcase with me. I'm not worried about changing the channel on the television because I know I'll need to board soon. I'm not worried about looking my best because, if I'm lucky, I'll sleep on the plane.

I know that when I get home, I'll get to see my family—I'll get to hug my wife and son. I know my wife will make her delicious homemade biscuits and turkey chili. I know that I'll be able to shower and relax and can sink into my comfortable, cozy chair that reclines. I know that the beach chairs in the backyard with some lemonade will help me unwind. I know my surfboards, clothes, car, books, and more are waiting for me at home whenever I want entertainment. My house is more cozy than any airport hotel, and my bed is more comfortable than any hotel bed. Any airport or airplane food is bearable because I just need to be sustained until I get home. I don't worry about how I sleep in the hotel airport if I miss my connection because I have to get up early anyway to catch the flight. I can go for small stretches away from my loved ones because I know I'll be reunited with them back home soon.

The parallels between an airport and our physical life on this side of eternity are striking. On earth, my objective isn't to make this life the most comfortable. I don't worry about what I will eat or wear. I don't focus on storing up treasures here on earth. I'm not supposed to spend my time and energy entertaining myself above all else. I'm not supposed to worry about gathering possessions. None of that matters in light of eternity. What matters is how I use this life, the treasure I store in heaven, the relationships I build, the souls I win, the lives that are forever changed, and the talents I steward. The same is true for you.

LIVING FOR THE PRIZE

As we shift our gaze to heaven, we are to operate with clarity and focus on the end state, our end goal, the perfecter of our faith. Having grown up playing sports, I love the way Paul phrases it in 1 Corinthians 9:24: "Do you not know that in a race all the runners run, but only one gets the prize? Run in such a way as to get the prize."

Let us run to win—not just to show up, compete, try, or have fun—but to win! The way we do this is by actively reminding ourselves that this life is not our forever home; heaven is. What we see now is only temporary. There is a home more real than the one we now see. There is a spiritual reality more permanent than this physical one. One day, we will have a heavenly body and shed the cocoon of our earthly bodies.

> So will it be with the resurrection of the dead. The body that is sown is perishable, it is raised imperishable; it is sown in dishonor, it is raised in glory; it is sown in weakness, it is raised in power; it is sown a natural body, it is raised a spiritual body. If there is a natural body, there is also a spiritual body. (1 Corinthians 15:42-44)

We must remind ourselves that Jesus is our reward. Jesus is our King. He is our prize and special treasure, and we are the reward of His suffering. Once we understand this, our view of earth and the material things around us changes drastically. We find ourselves losing passion for what we once chased after. Previous enjoyments that once fulfilled no longer provide satisfaction. Our lifestyle changes. The way we speak changes. The way we think changes.

> Do not conform to the pattern of this world, but be transformed by the renewing of your mind. Then you will be able to

test and approve what God's will is—his good, pleasing and perfect will. (Romans 12:2)

As we run with all of our might, we find that we slowly lose ourselves, yet also somehow find ourselves. As we decrease, Jesus increases (John 3:30), and we receive more than we had. It is in losing ourselves that we truly find our identity. And so, it is with our finances. As we grow in the spiritual fruits and disciplines of the Spirit-filled life, we gain a greater inheritance that can never perish, spoil, or fade.

> Praise be to the God and Father of our Lord Jesus Christ! In His great mercy, He has given us new birth into a living hope through the resurrection of Jesus Christ from the dead, and into an inheritance that can never perish, spoil, or fade. This inheritance is kept in heaven for you. (1 Peter 1:3-4)

I pray we have such eyes for heaven and are so captivated by the goodness of God and His eternal rewards that we move into a place where we long to be blessed in the heavenlies more than in the physical. I still find myself struggling with this. As I donate to charitable causes, give generously, and tithe regularly, all too often I find myself hoping for a return on my investment in this life. May we be a people so rooted in the Spirit that every financial seed we sow is aimed not at an earthly return but at an eternal reward in heaven.

A GENERATION ON FIRE

We live in a generation enamored with fame and the concept of getting rich quickly. Anywhere you look—on YouTube, Instagram, TikTok, or Facebook—you'll find someone sharing the five secrets to building passive income, the seven steps to making seven figures, or the ten steps to becoming a millionaire by thirty. The fascination with money is core to humanity, as Jesus Himself addresses this issue during His life on earth over two thousand years ago: "Again I tell you, it is easier for a camel to go through the eye of a needle than for someone who is rich to enter the kingdom of God" (Matthew 19:24).

Or more starkly, 1 Timothy 6:10 says, "For the love of money is a root of all kinds of evil. Some people, eager for money, have wandered from the faith and pierced themselves with many griefs."

So, *how are we to view money?* It isn't to be our desire, passion, or purpose in life to obtain it; instead, we are to be faithful stewards with what God provides, understanding that it is always His and never ours. The Bible speaks of money as a tool: "I tell you, use worldly wealth to gain friends for yourselves, so that when it is gone, you will be welcomed into eternal dwellings" (Luke 16:9).

As we grow our finances—money, stocks, portfolios, houses, possessions, and more—we are to do so with a kingdom perspective. Many men and women in the Bible were historically rich yet heroically faithful. My prayer is that we become more like these kinds of people. May our generation be so captivated by the goodness of God that we give recklessly to see the kingdom of God flourish. May we be a generation that handles earthly wealth with an eternal vision, investing not just in portfolios but in the kingdom that never fades. As culture twists this divine calling, may God's people be ones who shine like stars among a crooked and corrupt generation, found faithful in our whole house (Philippians 2:15).

I believe we are on the cusp of a generation that trusts Jesus so wholeheartedly, follows Him so faithfully, lives so wildly, walks so radically, and runs so freely that it shakes the earth. He is raising up godly doctors, lawyers, entertainers, educators, business leaders, engineers, artists, athletes, scientists, writers, chefs, musicians, nurses, architects, farmers, plumbers, electricians, designers, technicians, psychologists, and so many more who will honor Him with their lives.

Our generation has a chance to walk counter-culturally by

embracing the paradoxical truths of our spiritual life to see His kingdom come. We can be the generation that sees the first corporation give $1 billion to advance the kingdom of Jesus. We can be the generation to see missionaries no longer needing to fundraise, allowing them to focus entirely on their mission work. We can be the generation to see orphans and widows living in mansions, embraced by love and care. We can be the generation to see pastors no longer burdened by financial concerns but free to lead and inspire with passion.

We can be the generation to see all this happen if we will catch hold of the vision to live wildly generous and radically free—a life as abundant as Jesus longs to give each of us.

May we be these wildly generous types of people. These people, those who are truly found in Him, will be so faithful in the little things that God won't be able to help but bless them with much. And as God does, His name will be magnified, His words will be amplified, His love will be lifted high, and His bride will be glorified.

Our Lord, come (Maranatha)!

ABOUT THE AUTHOR & HOW TO GET INVOLVED

Jacob Cokely is dedicated to helping people live radically free and wildly generous through Jesus. From giving everything in his bank account to stewarding abundance, Jacob has experienced God's supernatural provision in every financial season. Through it all, giving has remained a priority, and abundance has followed. Though he works in the technology industry, his deepest passion is following Jesus wherever He leads. He lives in Southern California with his wife and son.

If you're ready to take the next step in living generously, Jacob has created practical resources to help you put Kingdom generosity into action for free at *www.kingdomgenerosity.podia.com*:

- **3-Day Devotional on Generosity**: A short, powerful guide to jumpstart your heart for giving.
- **30-Day Generosity Journey**: A full month of exercises, reflections, and challenges to help you steward your time, talents, and treasures.

Most importantly, it's time to share your generosity journey with others:

- Start sharing your story with family, friends, or your local church.
- Connect directly with Jacob by sending your testimony to *@jacob_cokely* on Instagram.

Kingdom Generosity is more than a book—it's a movement. Every step you take in faith, every act of giving, and every story you share helps extend God's Kingdom on earth. Join the movement, experience the abundant life, and inspire others to live generously as well.